D1512299

SOCIAL ISSUES
FIRSTHAND

Teenage Pregnancy

Other Books in the Social Issues Firsthand Series:

SOCIAL ISSUES
FIRSTHAND

Teenage Pregnancy

Norah Piehl, Book Editor

North Arkansas College
1515 Pioneer Drive
Harrison, AR 72601

GREENHAVEN PRESS
A part of Gale, Cengage Learning

GALE
CENGAGE Learning

Detroit • New York • San Francisco • New Haven, Conn • Waterville, Maine • London

GALE
CENGAGE Learning

Christine Nasso, *Publisher*
Elizabeth Des Chenes, *Managing Editor*

© 2009 Greenhaven Press, a part of Gale, Cengage Learning.

Gale and Greenhaven Press are registered trademarks used herein under license.

For more information, contact:
Greenhaven Press
27500 Drake Rd.
Farmington Hills, MI 48331-3535
Or you can visit our Internet site at gale.cengage.com

For product information and technology assistance, contact us at

Gale Customer Support, 1-800-877-4253
For permission to use material from this text or product, submit all requests online at www.cengage.com/permissions

Further permissions questions can be emailed to permissionrequest@cengage.com

Articles in Greenhaven Press anthologies are often edited for length to meet page requirements. In addition, original titles of these works are changed to clearly present the main thesis and to explicitly indicate the author's opinion. Every effort is made to ensure that Greenhaven Press accurately reflects the original intent of the authors. Every effort has been made to trace the owners of copyrighted material.

Cover image © Natalia Shmeliova. Image from BigStockPhoto.com.

LIBRARY OF CONGRESS CATALOGING-IN-PUBLICATION DATA

Teenage pregnancy / Norah Piehl, book editor.
    p. cm. -- (Social issues firsthand)
  Includes bibliographical references and index.
  ISBN 978-0-7377-4254-1 (hardcover)
  1. Teenage parents. 2. Teenage pregnancy. I. Piehl, Norah.
  HQ759.64.T38 2009
  306.8740835'0973--dc22
                               2008028519

Printed in the United States of America
1 2 3 4 5 6 7 12 11 10 09 08

Contents

Chapter 1: Teens Facing Pregnancy

Chapter 2: Growing Up While Raising a Child

Chapter 3: Professionals Helping Teen Parents

Foreword

Social issues are often viewed in abstract terms. Pressing challenges such as poverty, homelessness, and addiction are viewed as problems to be defined and solved. Politicians, social scientists, and other experts engage in debates about the extent of the problems, their causes, and how best to remedy them. Often overlooked in these discussions is the human dimension of the issue. Behind every policy debate over poverty, homelessness, and substance abuse, for example, are real people struggling to make ends meet, to survive life on the streets, and to overcome addiction to drugs and alcohol. Their stories are ubiquitous and compelling. They are the stories of everyday people—perhaps your own family members or friends—and yet they rarely influence the debates taking place in state capitols, the national Congress, or the courts.

The disparity between the public debate and private experience of social issues is well illustrated by looking at the topic of poverty. Each year the U.S. Census Bureau establishes a poverty threshold. A household with an income below the threshold is defined as poor, while a household with an income above the threshold is considered able to live on a basic subsistence level. For example, in 2003 a family of two was considered poor if its income was less than $12,015; a family of four was defined as poor if its income was less than $18,810. Based on this system, the bureau estimates that 35.9 million Americans (12.5 percent of the population) lived below the poverty line in 2003, including 12.9 million children below the age of eighteen.

Commentators disagree about what these statistics mean. Social activists insist that the huge number of officially poor Americans translates into human suffering. Even many families that have incomes above the threshold, they maintain, are likely to be struggling to get by. Other commentators insist that the statistics exaggerate the problem of poverty in the United States. Compared to people in developing countries, they point out, most so-called poor families have a high quality of life. As stated by journalist Fidelis Iyebote, "Cars are owned by 70 percent of 'poor' households. . . . Color televisions belong to 97 percent of the 'poor' [and] videocassette recorders belong to nearly 75 percent. . . . Sixty-four percent have microwave ovens, half own a stereo system, and over a quarter possess an automatic dishwasher."

However, this debate over the poverty threshold and what it means is likely irrelevant to a person living in poverty. Simply put, poor people do not need the government to tell them whether they are poor. They can see it in the stack of bills they cannot pay. They are aware of it when they are forced to choose between paying rent or buying food for their children. They become painfully conscious of it when they lose their homes and are forced to live in their cars or on the streets. Indeed, the written stories of poor people define the meaning of poverty more vividly than a government bureaucracy could ever hope to. Narratives composed by the poor describe losing jobs due to injury or mental illness, depict horrific tales of childhood abuse and spousal violence, recount the loss of friends and family members. They evoke the slipping away of social supports and government assistance, the descent into substance abuse and addiction, the harsh realities of life on the streets. These are the perspectives on poverty that are too often omitted from discussions over the extent of the problem and how to solve it.

Greenhaven Press's *Social Issues Firsthand* series provides a forum for the often-overlooked human perspectives on society's most divisive topics of debate. Each volume focuses on one social issue and presents a collection of ten to sixteen narratives by those who have had personal involvement with the topic. Extra care has been taken to include a diverse range of perspectives. For example, in the volume on adoption, readers will find the stories of birth parents who have made an adoption plan, adoptive parents, and adoptees themselves. After exposure to these varied points of view, the reader will have a clearer understanding that adoption is an intense, emotional experience full of joyous highs and painful lows for all concerned.

The debate surrounding embryonic stem cell research illustrates the moral and ethical pressure that the public brings to bear on the scientific community. However, while nonexperts often criticize scientists for not considering the potential negative impact of their work, ironically the public's reaction against such discoveries can produce harmful results as well. For example, although the outcry against embryonic stem cell research in the United States has resulted in fewer embryos being destroyed, those with Parkinson's, such as actor Michael J. Fox, have argued that prohibiting the development of new stem cell lines ultimately will prevent a timely cure for the disease that is killing Fox and thousands of others.

Each book in the series contains several features that enhance its usefulness, including an in-depth introduction, an annotated table of contents, bibliographies for further research, a list of organizations to contact, and a thorough index. These elements—combined with the poignant voices of people touched by tragedy and triumph—make the *Social Issues Firsthand* series a valuable resource for research on today's topics of political discussion.

Introduction

Fifteen-year-old Kate was at the top of her class, excelling at academics and athletics, with her eye on a college scholarship and a medical career. When Kate became pregnant as a sophomore in high school, however, her plans were thrown way off track. Although Kate's future was now far from certain, this high-achieving student was sure about one thing: "I couldn't leave school," she said in a November 11, 2005, article on teenwire.com. "It would be the end of my life." With the help of a low-cost, on-site child care service at the school she attended, Kate would be able to finish high school, care for her son, and even keep college as part of her long-range plans.

Schools for Pregnant and Parenting Teens: A Dying Breed?

Each year, close to half a million teenage girls in the United States have babies, according to a May 2006 report in the *Washington Times*, forcing many to face challenging realities and make difficult choices, just like Kate. However, one option that is open to fewer and fewer teenage parents is the availability of separate high school programs focused specifically on the needs of young parents. These alternative high schools, which often admit both pregnant and parenting students, almost always provide students free or low-cost child care services and, in addition to customary academic subjects, offer life skills classes on topics such as work–family balance, parenting techniques, and child development. Many also provide other services such as on-site prenatal or pediatric nursing services, transportation to and from school, legal services, housing and job assistance, expanded availability of mental health and family counselors, and dedicated social work staff.

Although these programs may sound wonderful on paper, and despite some evidence that these programs may help improve outcomes for teenage parents and their often at-risk children, they have, in recent years, faced closure at unprecedented rates. Alternative parenting schools have both fans and detractors, and both supporters and critics can build strong cases for the continuation—or closure—of these separate, but possibly unequal, programs.

"We Have Different Lives"

The Personal Responsibility and Work Opportunity Reconciliation Act of 1996 (better known as "welfare reform") requires teenage parents who wish to receive federal welfare assistance to live at home with parents and to stay in school as long as required by state law. As a result, many states have instituted laws mandating that school districts provide free or low-cost child care facilities as part of their regular high schools. So what are the benefits of providing separate facilities and programs for pregnant and parenting teens if child care facilities are already part of many mainstream school programs?

For one thing, argue supporters of these programs, the very same students who become teen parents are also the most likely to have other preexisting risk factors for dropping out of school, including living in poverty, having a family history of abuse, or being themselves the children of teenage parents. Teenage motherhood is also one of the largest risk factors for dropping out of school; according to a 2006 national study cited in the *Sarasota (Fla.) Herald-Tribune* in May 2008, one-third of teenage girls who did not graduate from high school dropped out because they became pregnant. Providing these high-risk students with additional tools and a supportive environment could possibly help further decrease the dropout rate in this vulnerable population and also potentially result in improved outcomes for their children. In addition, the availability in many teen parent programs of such medical services as prenatal care in a school setting could help reduce the public health problem of low-birth-weight and pre-term babies born to teenage mothers.

For many students and educators, however, the key factor in promoting the existence of these parenting programs is the mental and emotional well-being of the students involved. As one faculty mentor at a parenting program in Tempe, Arizona, explained in a September 2006 *Arizona Daily Star* article, "Sometimes you need someone who's just for you." This individualized attention and compassionate fulfillment of specific needs are also what attract many students to these programs, even when they have the opportunity to stay in a more traditional high school program. "They didn't cater to pregnant girls at all. . . . They don't have any sympathy for you," remarked one seventeen-year-old student about her initial experience at a mainstream public school, in a March 2006 *Baltimore Sun* article. In the Fall 2007 issue of *American Secondary Education*, another student argued that her original high school "didn't understand that we have different lives than the other students. We have different responsibilities." Recognition, and respect, of those different responsibilities seems to be what attracts many students to these special programs and keeps them there either until they have gained the confidence and skills required to succeed in a mainstream school or until graduation.

No Special Treatment

Other students, however, resent being singled out for special treatment just because of their identity as pregnant or parenting teens. One student quoted in a May 2008 *Sarasota Herald-Tribune* article said that "I wanted to be in a regular high school with regular people. I didn't want to be treated like I was any different." In addition to student concerns about being marginalized, some members of the educational and general communities worry that providing such specialized services to young parents serves as an implicit stamp of approval of teenage pregnancy and childbirth. In a letter to the editor reprinted in the Fall 2007 issue of *American Secondary Education*, one community member expressed his disapproval of his town's parenting program, writing, "By providing venues such as these, we are enabling and possibly encouraging bad choices and a lack of personal responsibility."

Having community support of these facilities is key. Because of their high costs, which can be upward of $23,000 per student per the *Sarasota Herald-Tribune*, many school districts seek community funding for services above and beyond the traditional academic subjects that are provided for by taxpayer dollars. In 2006, one teen parenting program appealed to taxpayers to donate directly to their $15,000 budget shortfall, in addition to soliciting private donations and institutional grants.

Critics of these programs often point out that in addition to being costly, teen parenting programs and other alternative schools fail to live up to the more rigorous academic standards set by their traditional counterparts. Ambitious students are often disappointed by the slower pace and limited subjects offered by programs for teen parents, and they may need to supplement their education by, for example, taking classes at community colleges. Less motivated students may have other problems. One Florida school for teenage parents was closed following its repeated failure to live up to national standards set by the No Child Left Behind Act. What's more, more than a decade of steadily falling teenage birth rates have resulted in steadily falling enrollment in specialty teenage parenting programs, some of which serve only a few dozen students.

A final criticism of these schools posited by their detractors is that many of these schools were founded at a time when teenage pregnancy, and unwed motherhood in general, was highly stigmatized. Now, however, with teen parenthood achieving high levels of visibility, in, for example, the 2007 hit movie *Juno*, critics argue that removing pregnant and parenting students from their mainstream high schools—from their usual friends and classes—is no longer necessary or appropriate. With their high cost, low enrollment, potentially less rigorous academic standards, and perceived irrelevance, is it any wonder that separate teenage parenting programs are facing closure at unprecedented rates?

Looking Forward

Students, teachers, administrators, and the community at large may not agree on the best way to educate teenagers who have children. Most observers of the situation, however, are unanimous in their support of allowing these students to remain in public schooling—whatever form it takes—and in their desire to offer a better start for the young children of these teen parents. Although teenage birth rates had previously declined for the past dozen years or more, the rate did rise 3 percent in 2006, according to a study cited in the December 7, 2007, *New York Times*, indicating that the problem of teenage pregnancy is far from solved and that educating teenage parents and caring for their children are challenges that will continue to face the United States for many years to come.

CHAPTER 1

Teens Facing Pregnancy

Forced to Give Up Their Babies

Nancy Horgan, Lydia Manderson, and Susan Souza

Prior to the availability of safe, legal abortions and the advent of open adoptions, teenage girls who got pregnant had few choices. In the 1950s and 1960s, teen pregnancy was far more stigmatized than it is today, and pregnant teens were sources of shame for their parents, their schools, and their communities.

Here, three women who had babies as teenagers in the 1960s tell their stories. All three were sent by their families to maternity homes for the final months of their pregnancies. There the girls gave birth and immediately gave their babies up for adoption, often without the opportunity to hold, touch, or even see their newborns.

The women, now in their fifties, all speak of the shame and fear they felt as a result of their pregnancies, as well as the harsh treatment they experienced in the maternity homes. Their stories speak to the long-lasting effects on the birth mother of giving away a baby for adoption so abruptly; all three searched for, and eventually found, the children they had been forced to give away.

The stories of these women, along with more than one hundred others like them, are collected in Ann Fessler's book The Girls Who Went Away.

Teenage pregnancy is a complex and often emotionally charged issue. Suddenly the teens—usually with their parents—are faced with difficult choices: Should the girl get married or, perhaps, raise the child on her own? Maybe she would prefer adoption—the kind where she can select the child's parent. Then again, she may choose to terminate the pregnancy. Girls didn't always have so many options. Before the introduction of the birth control pill and the sexual revolution of the '60s, before *Roe v. Wade*—the 1973 Supreme Court decision that legalized abortion—and before there was open discussion of adoption, a girl "in trouble" typically followed a single path: She waited out the pregnancy at a no-frills maternity home, then surrendered her child for adoption. In her new book *The Girls Who Went Away*, Ann Fessler, a 56-year-old adoptee, talked to more than 100 of the estimated 1.5 million women . . . gave up their babies in the '50s, '60s and early '70s, only to return home and pretend the births had never happened. Three of these women spoke to *People* about their experiences and their reunions with children they never thought they would see again.

Nancy Horgan, 56

She asked to hold her baby just for a minute. No, said the nurse.

When my parents sent me to the Sophia Little Home in Cranston, R.I., I was 17 and seven months pregnant by my boyfriend, a 19-year-old sailor. The youngest girl there was 14 and the oldest was 22. I spent the next two months doing arts and crafts. We were told not to tell each other our last names. We never talked about what was going to happen to our bodies. There was no help to prepare us for the grief that was to lie ahead.

The birth was humiliating. I was dropped off at the hospital entirely on my own. After laboring alone all night, I was taken to a big room and strapped to the delivery table. In the lamp over my head I could see the reflection of the child being born. When they noticed that I would see, they tipped it away; the child was for them to see, not for me.

I named the baby Chris and asked every day to see him. A social worker said, "I have these papers, and your father wants them signed now." In a file she wrote, "We are going to have problems with this girl. She talks about that baby all the time." Several days after the birth, the head of the hospital showed up. I said, "You can't keep me from him. He's mine." She said, "Yes, unfortunately he is, and let's hope it doesn't happen again." Some woman put me in a wheelchair and pushed me up to the nursery window. I asked, "Can I hold him?" She said, "No. Are you done?" Then the social worker took Chris away. Back at home, we never discussed that I had had a baby. But I always had the idea that I would start looking for my child when he was 18. I told my husband three months before we married, "I have a child who is going to be part of my life someday." He was like, "Cool."

But I realized I was afraid of my son: What if he is mean, or mad that I did this? When an intermediary located Kurt (the name given by the couple who had adopted him), he was 21. I was not ready for seeing a full-grown adult. At our first meeting, I told him, "You know, they never let me touch you." Afterward I fell apart. I couldn't work or sleep for six months; all I did was cry. I couldn't believe that I had let my parents do this to me. I started seeing a psychiatrist. It was devastating to realize I had no voice at all over something so life-changing as having a child. Today, Kurt and I have a close relationship. Looking back, I just wish I had been older. Then I would have had the power to resist.

Lydia Manderson, 55

Meeting her son—and the couple who raised him—was momentous.

It was 1968 in Simi Valley, Calif. I was 16 and dating Tony. We decided we needed to tell our parents that I was pregnant. We waited probably longer than we should have; I think I was 10 weeks along. My parents had Tony's parents come over. In those days, if you were pregnant and not married, you weren't an "expectant mother." I was an "unwed mother," which had a serious stigma. It meant that I was promiscuous and the baby was "illegitimate." I knew I wasn't anything like that—I had never been intimate with anyone before my boyfriend—and "illegitimate" conjured up a lot of images: lower-class, trashy families. I felt like I was shaming my baby.

My parents made the decision for me to go to a home. I never remember feeling for a second that it was my choice. And I had never been away from home before. I was terrified. The home was run by the Salvation Army, with a long, dorm-like room. There had to have been 20 beds in it. Our names weren't used, so you had to listen for your number called over the loudspeaker. I was No. 4552—like an inmate. I was checked for STDs because it was assumed I had them. It was so insulting. I was so miserable. My dad finally came and got me, but it wasn't a good scene. Back home, I had to lock the door to my room. At one point he threw me across the living room. My mom was angry too that I was pregnant and living in her home. It wasn't until I was about 30 that I found out she was adopted! She saw in me the same situation her mother was once in. Later she told me she didn't want to find her birth mother because she didn't want to be rejected again. "That bitch better not show up at my door," she said, and she had the most furious look on her face I had ever seen.

My parents took me to the hospital. It was the same day astronauts first landed on the moon, and my dad left to go watch that on TV. Michael was born at 11:30 that night. I got to see him, and that was really important to me. I did get to hold him. But to keep me from bonding with the baby, the hospital kept me tethered to the bed with a catheter for five days and blatantly lied, telling me he was in an incubator. A few weeks later I went to the county clerk's office to sign papers. My parents took me and Tony. I had a little blanket and thought, "We'll pass this along to our son's new parents." And I remember the lady saying, "They won't be needing the blanket." When we came out of that office, my dad tried to put his arm around me. I distinctly remember jerking my shoulder away. I thought, the innocence is gone, my youth is gone.

In 1999, Michael tracked down my name and mother's address and left his contact information. I was cautious. I called a lawyer, and we did a DNA test. Then I called Tony, his father. We lived together for a year after the birth, but we couldn't put it behind us. We both married other people but reunited to meet our son and then to meet the people who raised him. It was momentous. I'm very aware that he has a mother and father who raised him, and they're his family. And yet we do have this relationship, and I can never just be his friend. I have to temper my instincts to smother him, but it doesn't mean that I don't have those feelings. I never had other children. I felt that it would almost be a betrayal of Mike. Now I need to make whatever concessions I have to, because I want him to feel comfortable. I lost this relationship so many years ago, and now here it is—what I've always wanted. It has come back to me.

Susan Souza, 55

Her dad wasn't going to allow his daughter to be labeled a bad girl.

I was madly in love with my boyfriend. When I got pregnant at 16, my parents were surprisingly supportive. They never belittled me; there was never any yelling. They invited him and his parents over to discuss the situation. When he said he wouldn't marry me, their plan for him to get a job and for me to take care of the baby fell apart. I thought I was the only one whose boyfriend didn't marry her. How ashamed I was, how embarrassed. The priest at our Catholic church had the situation all figured out. This happened routinely. I hid my pregnancy under tent dresses and finished my junior year of high school. At seven months, I was sent to St. Mary's Home for Unwed Mothers in Dorchester, Mass. My parents decided I would tell my boyfriend I'd had a miscarriage and made up stories to cover my absence—that I was working as a camp counselor; that I had mononucleosis.

My mother, best friend and cousin visited me. But when I went into labor, I was totally alone in my room until a nun took me to the hospital. She didn't say "goodbye" or "good luck." Nothing. No one had told me what to expect. It was very frightening. I was allowed to hold and feed my baby girl, whom I named Madlyn, after my mother. But in the end I was given no choice. My father was a policeman; his word was law in our house. Dad wasn't going to allow his daughter to be labeled a bad girl or his granddaughter a bastard. I know he wanted the best for me and for her. But when I signed those papers, I knew that wasn't right. I might have been 17, but I would have been a good mother.

I went back to high school and my boyfriend, but I never told him what I had been through. Years later, I ran into him and we had a cup of coffee. I told him about our daughter. He was very blase. As for myself, I eventually married, had two daughters, got divorced, then remarried and had another daughter. I'd always planned to search for Madlyn when she was 21, but then my daughter Jacqueline died of leukemia and I was grieving. When I was 47, I started looking, at first on the Internet. When that didn't work, my husband suggested a private investigator, who found her in two weeks. I spent weeks composing a letter. I waited weeks to call, and when I did, she seemed wary. She had a good life and great parents. But I didn't care what her tone was. I just wanted to keep her talking. She agreed to a meeting, and I drove the housekeeper crazy that day. I wanted everything to be perfect. When she walked up the stairs of this house, I just . . . it's indescribable. I just couldn't stop hugging and kissing her. The best part was, she was kissing me back.

I never confronted my father about sending me away; it wouldn't have served a purpose. But after his death my mother admitted she felt guilty. I didn't realize until she said "I'm sorry" that I was looking for that. Those words were very powerful.

I Hid My Pregnancy

Diana, as told to Whitney Joiner

Diana was a sophomore in high school when she got pregnant. She and her boyfriend had been together for more than a year when she began to suspect that she was pregnant—despite the fact that she and her boyfriend had consistently used birth control. Raised in a strict Catholic household in a conservative community, Diana was terrified to tell her parents about her pregnancy.

Despite professing a desire for an abortion, Diana waited until it was too late to obtain one, and then spent the next several months hiding her pregnancy from her family and friends until just days before giving birth.

Diana's story of isolation, fear, and shame illustrates the need for pregnant teens to find trustworthy adults in whom to confide during their pregnancies. By keeping her secret to herself, Diana lost out on both receiving prenatal care for herself and her baby and obtaining vital emotional support during this time.

My family spent a lot of time together when I was growing up in Pasadena, California. The local Catholic community was important to my mom and dad, so we all went to church every Sunday and attended church gatherings too. At the time I'd never had a boyfriend. I was a virgin—and thought I would be until I got married.

Young Love

One afternoon in October 2002, during my freshman year of high school, I dressed up like a fairy for our school's costume day. Sitting in class, I saw a hot guy, Ely, a junior who had just

Diana, as told to Whitney Joiner, "I Hid My Pregnancy!" *Seventeen*, vol. 65, no. 12, December 2006, pp. 104, 106. Reproduced by permission.

transferred in. At the end of the period, he stopped by my desk. "You look really pretty," he said. "Thanks," I responded, and smiled. I was so excited that he'd noticed me!

After that, Ely and I started talking every day in class about our families, friends, and the kind of music and movies we liked. When he asked me to be his girlfriend four months later, I immediately said yes. We started hanging out after school and going shopping or to the movies each weekend. On Sundays he even came to church with me and my family.

My parents really liked Ely, but they didn't allow us to be alone in my room. Since his parents weren't as strict, we'd go to his house to make out. I had told Ely early on that I was a virgin, so he never pressured me. One day I asked him if he'd ever had sex, and he told me yes—once, with his last girlfriend.

Then in November 2003, after we'd been together for nine months, Ely and I were hooking up in his room, and in the heat of the moment, we decided to have sex. "We should use a condom," Ely suggested, and I agreed. So we used protection then—and every other time we had sex. I thought about going on birth control, but I figured the doctor would tell my mom—and I was so afraid she'd be disappointed in me.

Tough Situation

One Saturday morning three months later, I woke up feeling sick to my stomach. *That's weird*, I thought. *But I can't be pregnant—we always use condoms.* That afternoon I was watching TV when I remembered that I was supposed to have gotten my period—and hadn't! *Did one of the condoms break and we didn't realize it?* I started to panic.

"I think I might be pregnant," I told Ely the next morning. "Really?" he said, sounding excited. I couldn't believe he seemed *happy*. *Does he actually think we're ready to be parents?* I thought. "Let's go to Planned Parenthood and get a test to make sure," he said. For the next few days, while I waited for my appointment, I tried to stay busy to keep it out of my mind.

At Planned Parenthood they gave me a test—and I *was* pregnant. I was terrified! "You're probably due in September," the nurse said. "Do you plan to keep it or terminate it?" Ely looked at me, and without thinking I said, "Terminate it." Ely said he'd call a clinic—but a few days later he still hadn't. "Did you call today?" I asked. "Yeah, but no one picked up the phone," he said. I kept asking him, but each time he had an excuse. He didn't say so, but I suspected that he wanted to keep the baby. I didn't—and I know it sounds crazy, but it *still* hadn't occurred to me to make the call myself. I was so overwhelmed by the thought of having a baby and being a mom that I forced myself to not even think about it.

In April, when I was four months pregnant, I finally called and made an appointment to get the abortion. But by the time the date came, we still didn't know how much it would cost or how to get there (the clinic was 10 miles away). So we simply didn't go.

Truth Revealed

Meanwhile I had gained almost 20 pounds—and none of my clothes fit me anymore. Since my sisters were bigger, I just borrowed their stuff. But my family *did* start commenting about my weight. In July 2004, when I was seven months pregnant, one of my aunts took me aside and said, "I noticed that you're getting big. Are you pregnant?" Scared, I shot back, "Of course not! I don't know *why* I'm gaining weight!" She seemed to believe me, but after that, I tried not to leave the house as much so no one would notice. A few weeks later my mom sat me down. "You're not acting like yourself. Are you okay?" she asked. "I'm just upset that I'm gaining weight and can't seem to take it off," I replied. The truth is, I wanted to tell my mom because I was lonely and crying all the time. I wanted her and my sisters to help me, but I was too scared to let them know—I thought they would be so disappointed in me.

By early August my face was huge, my feet were swollen, and without baggy clothes on, I definitely looked eight months pregnant. I started worrying about my health—and the baby's—since I hadn't seen a doctor. I tried to work up the courage to tell my mom, but again I lost my nerve, knowing how upset she would be.

The next month I was watching TV one day when my mom and dad—who once had said jokingly that I looked pregnant—sat beside me. "We want to know what's going on," my mom said. "Are you pregnant?" my dad asked. I was so tired of keeping it a secret that I burst into tears and nodded. They were surprised, and I could see in my dad's face that he was angry, but they didn't yell at me. "Why didn't you tell us?" my mom asked. "I was afraid you'd be upset with me," I sobbed. I was just so relieved to finally have the truth out in the open.

Important Lesson

The next day was Labor Day, and since medical offices were closed, my mom wanted to take me to the emergency room to see a doctor. But my aunt was having a barbecue, and I didn't want everyone to wonder why we weren't there. So I asked my mom if we could go to the hospital afterward.

During the cookout I started to get sharp pains in my stomach. I told my mom and she said, "You're probably having contractions!" She started timing my pains, and once they were six minutes apart we went to the hospital. At 7:32 A.M. on September 7, 2004, I gave birth to a girl. We combined my name and Ely's and named her Illiana.

A year later Ely and I broke up. Now Illiana and I live with my parents, and Ely visits her every day. Being a single mom is *really* hard. I work full-time *and* go to school full-time. I couldn't do it without my parents—but I really regret not turning to them for help sooner.

A Desperate Choice

Twyana Davis, as told to Stephanie Booth

*Twyana Davis had always been a "good girl," excelling in school
and performing well in sports. When she became pregnant just
before her first year in college, she was terrified of disappointing
her family and tarnishing her image. Frightened, isolated, and
ashamed, she wound up not only hiding her pregnancy and giving birth alone but also hiding her newborn daughter in a dumpster outside her college dorm room before alerting the police to
the abandoned child.*

*Davis's story calls attention to the increasing availability of
so-called "safe havens," public places such as hospitals and fire-
houses where desperate mothers can leave their babies safely,
without fear of harm to their babies or prosecution for themselves. Almost all states now have laws mandating availability of
these safe havens.*

*After her brief moment of desperation, Davis admitted what
she had done to her daughter and worked with her grandparents
and authorities to reclaim custody of her child. Eventually, Davis
did regain custody and went on to found a nonprofit organization dedicated to reducing the incidence of infant abandonment.
She also wrote a best selling memoir,* Sacred Womb, *about her
experiences, and appeared on the* Oprah Winfrey Show *to tell
her story.*

Five years ago [in 1997] two policemen showed up at my
home on Thanksgiving. Days earlier a newborn had been
found in a dumpster outside my dorm at Ohio Dominican
College, in Columbus, Ohio. Since I'd been one of the few
people left on campus then, they wanted to know if I'd seen
anything.

Twyana Davis, as told to Stephanie Booth, "She Threw Away Her Baby," *Teen People*,
vol. 5, no. 4, May 1, 2002, p. 122. Copyright © 2002 Time, Inc.. Reproduced by permission.

The story had been on TV nonstop. It's all my family could talk about—how cute the baby girl was and how could anyone do such a terrible thing. It made me scared and sad to think about it, so I tuned it out.

At the police station I was taken into an interview room while my grandfather waited outside. The detectives were asking me routine questions when I suddenly started sobbing. "It's my daughter," I told them. "I left her there."

A Good Girl

I'm sure no one had suspected that the baby in the dumpster was mine. In high school I got good grades and played sports. I didn't date much and was embarrassed I hadn't done "it" by senior year. So that March, I lost my virginity to a guy I'd gone out with a few times. I was so naive; when the condom broke and he acted like it was no big deal, I believed him.

Two months later I knew I was pregnant. My body felt different, and I was constantly exhausted. I worked up the nerve to tell the guy, but he just didn't want to deal with it. I was scared my grandparents would feel the same. I'd lived with them since I was 14; they were loving but strict and eager for me to succeed. When we'd talked about sex, they'd just said, half-kidding, "Don't get pregnant or we'll put you out." No way did I want to let them down.

It's like I became two different people. Part of me went to class, played basketball and attended graduation. The other part did research on how my body was changing. I didn't show much until the fall. Then I hid my stomach by wearing baggy clothes. My college was just a few miles from my grandparents' house, but I didn't know anyone who went there. My roommate and I never saw each other, and I didn't try to make new friends.

A Lonely Birth

Just before Thanksgiving vacation, campus emptied out. I stayed for a late exam and was in my dorm room packing when my water broke. The contractions felt like being socked in the stomach. Two hours later, on a comforter on the floor, I gave birth to my daughter.

I was shaking and crying as I held her. What was I supposed to do? Why hadn't I told anyone? I felt like I was standing outside myself, watching a stranger clean off the baby and wrap her in a flannel shirt. I was so exhausted and in pain that I lay down next to her. Next thing I knew, I woke up at one in the morning.

Fear and Relief

My aunt was coming to pick me up that day, and I started panicking. My thoughts were totally irrational: Could I leave the baby there over the vacation? Could I secretly raise her in the dorm room? I remember thinking, "I've messed up big time." My only solution was to get rid of the baby. I never, ever wanted my baby to die—I just didn't know what to do. She was sleeping as I went down the stairs and, trying not to look at her tiny face, tucked her into a dumpster behind my dorm.

I called campus security as soon as I got back upstairs. Anonymously, I said I'd heard noises outside and described exactly where I'd put my daughter. Then I stood at the window and waited for the guard to show. The last feeling I had before passing out again was relief. My baby would be cared for. Everything would be back to normal.

Once I confessed to the police, my grandfather came into the room. Instead of being angry, he was in tears, telling me how bad he felt that I'd thought I couldn't come to him. "Do you want to keep this baby?" he asked. With him behind me, it finally felt OK to say yes.

My grandparents supported me 150 percent. They gained custody of my daughter, whom I named Danielle, and insisted I go back to school. I was expecting people to ignore me or call me names, but I got support and love from everyone. The first few times I visited Danielle, it was with a social worker. It was weird at first. I felt so sorry for what I'd done and so grateful that no harm had come to her. But I wondered, could I be a good mother? The more I saw Danielle, the more I realized how lucky I was.

A Second Chance

It took nearly a year before my case went to court. I was facing a possible 10-year prison sentence, and the judge had a reputation for being tough. The day of the sentencing, I pleaded guilty, and then stood and spoke from my heart, apologizing for what I'd done. When the judge gave me a year of house arrest and five years' probation, I couldn't believe it. I'd been given a second chance.

From that point on I felt like my life should be about helping others. I graduated from college and in 2000, my friend Love Ali and I started 2nd Chance of Life, a nonprofit organization dedicated to reducing infant abandonment. I didn't have anyone to confide in when I was pregnant; if I had, maybe none of this would have happened.

Thanks to my grandparents, I've also regained custody of Danielle, who's now five. She knows I "help moms with their babies." When she's older, I'll tell her the whole story. Until then, I just want to prevent as many teens as possible from making the same mistake I did.

Nine Months of Secrecy

Samantha Rice, as told to Stephanie Booth

Samantha was a sixteen-year-old high-school junior with a brand-new driver's license. Her exploration of her newfound freedom turned dangerous when she was raped by a man she met while out cruising with her friends. When she discovered she was pregnant, she felt she couldn't admit that she had been raped because she was afraid of what people in her small town might say about her. And since she was raised to believe that abortion was wrong, she decided that her only option was to keep her pregnancy a secret.

Samantha got some information about pregnancy from books, but never visited a doctor. She didn't gain much weight, so she was able to keep the pregnancy a secret from everyone, including her immediate family, right up until she went into labor. Her daughter was born a block away from the hospital.

The impact of her decision hit Samantha when she held her daughter in her arms for the first time. While she accepted the responsiblity of being a parent, she admits that she doesn't live a normal teenager's life. She also recognizes that she put her baby's health at risk by not telling anyone about the pregnancy. Samantha plans to become a nurse one day and hopes to help other teenage girls facing pregnancy.

If someone had come up to me last spring and said, "Samantha, by this time next year you'll be a mom," I would have told them they were crazy. I was an honor student. I didn't have a serious boyfriend. I was no more ready to be a mother than any other normal 16-year-old girl.

It happened in my junior year of high school. My friends and I could finally drive—suddenly we had all this freedom.

Samantha Rice, as told to Stephanie Booth, "9 Months of Secrecy," *Teen* Magazine, December 1998. Reproduced by permission.

We cruised around our small Colorado town looking for stuff to do. One night we met these cute guys from out of town. We had fun showing them around, and one guy asked if he could see me again.

"Sure," I said. He seemed nice enough.

The next night, I drove to the motel where he was staying. We started watching a movie, but he ended up raping me. I tried to stop him, but he forced himself on me. Afterward, I was so ashamed and depressed, I decided to pretend it never happened.

I'd missed my period before when I got stressed out, so at first I didn't freak when it didn't come. It took me three months to work up the courage to buy a pregnancy test. When I saw the little pink line that meant I was pregnant, thousands of thoughts shot through my head. I was shocked and angry, and even though I was close to both my parents, I couldn't bring myself to tell them. I knew how disappointed they'd be. I didn't think I'd be able to stand the looks on their faces.

Choosing Silence

It sounds crazy, but the only way I could deal with being pregnant was by not telling a soul. I couldn't tell people I had been raped, knowing everybody would be whispering about me. I didn't think about an abortion—I'd been raised to believe that it wasn't an option. I decided that when the baby was born, I would put it up for adoption. Until then, it would be my secret.

I worried that I would blow up like a balloon, but during the next six months I only gained about 10 pounds. No one noticed. When I was at seven months, my sister got married and I changed into my bridesmaid dress right in front of her. She didn't have a clue. But I certainly felt pregnant. I was tired all the time, and my ankles swelled up. I craved chocolate, pickles and really salty food.

Dating wasn't a problem—after I was raped, I stayed away from guys. The hard thing was concentrating on schoolwork. I'd always been a good student and didn't want to jeopardize that, so I forced myself to do homework and go to class.

I learned about pregnancy from an encyclopedia and books from health class. I knew not to drink alcohol or smoke, and I figured out myself when I was due. I never went to the doctor, though, which I now know was a huge mistake.

Giving Birth

My contractions started in school, at about 1:30 in the afternoon. The pain was like nothing I'd ever felt before: It was like being socked hard in the stomach. I said I was sick, and my teacher excused me. From that point, it was like I was on automatic pilot. I drove home, lay down on my bed and just dealt with the pain. It seemed like it would never end.

When my mom got home at 6:30, my contractions were closer together. "Are you OK?" she asked, sticking her head in my door.

"Just cramps," I said.

She nodded and closed the door, but I guess she didn't believe me, because she came back a few minutes later. By then my water had broken—the release of fluid that happens when the baby is about to be born—and I had to tell her.

Everything happened so fast. My dad pulled into the driveway just as Mom and I were leaving the house. She helped me into the back seat of his car and told him to drive to the hospital. My dad kept saying, "What's going on?" We were going 60 miles an hour across town when the baby's head started coming out. Thank God my mom knew what to do.

My daughter Bree was born one block away from the hospital. When we got to the emergency room, a doctor cut the umbilical cord and looked both of us over. We were both fine physically, but my parents were very worried and upset. I don't know how well I explained everything, but I told them I would give the baby up for adoption.

Yet when I held Bree in my arms, I knew I couldn't give her up. It was so amazing—she looked exactly like me! Suddenly, I realized how powerful it is to be a parent, even though I was still a kid.

Being a Parent

While I was in the hospital, I called my best friend. She was angry that I hadn't told her earlier. Looking back, I see she was right. I took a big risk not telling anyone, and especially not getting prenatal care. Every day I'm so grateful that my fear of seeking help didn't harm my baby.

Anyone who thinks having a baby is easy needs a reality check. I love Bree with all of my heart, but my life has completely changed since she was born.

At first I was overwhelmed. When we came home from the hospital, we didn't have anything—no crib, no clothes, no diapers. I took some time off from school to get used to being a mother, but when I went back, my mom quit her job to take care of Bree during the day. Now I come straight home from school every afternoon and take over from there.

When I returned to school, I got right back on the honor roll. My friends and teachers and even kids I didn't know too well were all cool to me. They wanted to see pictures of Bree. One day I brought her into my English class for an oral presentation about my life.

Still, it's weird being a mom and a teenager. I hardly go out with friends, and forget about dating! Few guys my age are into a girl with a baby. And I never, ever think about Bree's father.

After I graduate from high school, I plan to enroll in community college and study to become a registered nurse. I'd love to be able to help girls who are as scared and confused as I once was.

Becoming a Teenage Dad

Louis Desjarlais, as told to Nichole Huck

The following interview grew out of a class project coordinated by journalism college students in Canada. They sat down with a group of high school–age parents and encouraged the students to tell their own stories and to interview one another.

One story in particular caught the attention of journalism student Nichole Huck. Louis Desjarlais found out in ninth grade that he was going to be a father. He had been in trouble since his preteen years, selling drugs and spending time on the rough streets.

In this interview, which consists of his classmates' questions and Louis's answers, Louis explains how having a son eventually turned his troubled life around. After dropping out of school, Louis struggled with alcoholism but turned his behavior around when he realized his son needed the money more than Louis needed to drink. Louis's answers reveal his affection for his son but also the hard work and pressures involved in having a child at such a young age.

Nichole Huck graduated from the University of Regina School of Journalism and is now working in Northern Ghana with the nonprofit group Journalists for Human Rights.

O ver the last month [in spring 2005] a few journalism students from the University of Regina worked with a group of young parents at Cochrane High School.

In keeping with the principles of true community media, the parents were encouraged to tell their own stories and interview each other.

The class really opened up with one another and shared their experiences, but one story in particular gives a voice to a group that is seldom heard from in the media—young fathers.

Finding Out

How did you feel when you first found out you were going to be a dad?

I was in school at the time and when I heard that, I was really scared. I didn't know what to do. I wanted to help the mother and support the baby so I dropped out of school. I got a job, gave her money every two weeks. We had it going on, then she cheated on me.

Were you living together then?

Yeah, we had our own house and everything.

Where were you working?

I had jobs all over the streets and I was hustling the streets cause I was a bad guy at the time.

What do you mean hustling?

Selling drugs, buying stuff and selling it off for more.

Were you doing that to support your family?

Yeah, in a way, but I was doing that since I was 12.

Turning Things Around

Why did you decide this wasn't appropriate for you?

I don't have a charge on me. I have the cleanest record. I don't want to screw it up over something stupid.

You had been out of school for a while, what happened?

I dropped out in grade nine when I started having kids. Then two years ago I tried to come back to school but that didn't work out because I had a job too and they kept calling me back, and I needed the money. Last year I tried to come back again and then my brother passed away. It was really hard—I just wanted to drink and drink.

Do you feel your kids helped you through it?

Oh yeah, for sure. That's what helped me stop drinking. My baby needed money and I was spending it on beer. If I didn't have my baby, I'd probably be in jail.

What does being a dad mean to you?

It means a lot, like I can't even explain it. It's an awesome experience. It's a lot of money, but it's worth it. It's very worth it.

SOCIAL ISSUES
FIRSTHAND

CHAPTER 2

Growing Up While Raising a Child

Not Your Typical Teenage Mom

Jessica Allan

At the age of nineteen, Jessica Allan was married with one adopted child and a second one on the way. She had graduated from high school, served in the military, and attended college. Her pregnancy was not the result of a youthful indiscretion or a birth control failure; she and her husband actively tried to have a child. As she relates in this essay, she felt pride in her accomplishments and in her ability to avoid the state- and federal-subsidized programs that so many young parents rely on. So when Allan saw another young woman, close to her in age, at the obstetrician's waiting room, she had a hard time feeling sympathy or a sense of common ground with this more "typical" teenage mother.

Allan's essay reflects on society's judgmental attitude toward young parents, a prejudice she realizes she participates in. It also ultimately concludes that mothers—regardless of their age—have more in common than they might at first realize. Allan criticizes her own superiority complex and advocates that all parents provide support for each other in what is always a difficult job, regardless of individual circumstances.

Glancing around my obstetrician's clinic, I saw another young girl, perhaps seventeen years old. And my first thought was, "I am not you."

I was not a teenaged mother.

Sure, I was nineteen. Sure, this was my second child.

But damn it, I wasn't a teenaged mother.

Every qualification I could think of didn't apply to me.

Jessica Allan, "I Am Not You—Yes I Am," *Girl-Mom*, December 10, 2003. http://www.girl-mom.com/node/44. Reproduced by permission.

Atypical Credentials

I was married. I had another child, yes, and she was born when I was fifteen, yes, but she was my adopted stepdaughter. I had been to college. I had been in the army. My husband and I owned a house. I owned my own car, which was insured. I had health insurance, and a Visa card, and savings I could draw off of. I was a stay-at-home mother, my husband's and my choice.

I had grown up middle class, educated in private schools, and I had been attending college two weeks after my older daughter had been born, unbeknownst to me. I had military experience, and emergency medical technician credentials. I chose not to work.

I volunteered at a local hospital and made charitable donations to the Salvation Army and the United Way. I was not on AFDC [Aid to Families with Dependent Children]. I met none of the "low-trajectory" qualifications named in Kristen Luker's book *Dubious Conceptions*. I had read the book in college and found it interesting, if at the time irrelevant to my own life.

Neither Poor Nor Miserable

I was not a teenaged mother.

I didn't have a low-paying job at Wal-Mart. I had a G.E.D. [general equivalency diploma], by accident of having gone to college early. I was married. I was not on WIC [government supplemental nutrition program], Medicaid, AFDC, or food stamps. I had an education. I didn't have a boyfriend who beat me and drank the rent money. I even had to take clomiphene [a drug that induces ovulation] to get pregnant—if there's one way to confirm that a pregnancy was "intended," it's to take fertility drugs to make it happen.

Unlike this poor, miserable creature sitting in the waiting room, I was not a teenaged mother.

Nothing in Common

She and I were the only young women under the age of 25 or so in the waiting room. As I watched her, fascinated with her morbid situation, I saw a tear slip off of her cheek and drop onto the copy of *Parents* magazine that she was reading.

Damn it. I have nothing in common with you. Don't make me pity your situation. Damn it, damn it, damn it. I knew my empathy would be the end of me.

And, girding myself, I walked over, sat down and introduced myself.

Her story I won't relate here, for it is hers and not mine. But it was no more "typical" than mine. No story is typical. They are all the combination of accidents of fate and choice over circumstance, and it is too horrible to categorize one as "typical."

A Lonely Life

Once I married a man with a two-year-old daughter, my friends from college hastily decamped. They quickly predicted that I would become a complete drudge and no fun to be around.

They may well have been right. I try not to think of how true that very well was, being a housewife and mother. And, in my reluctance to find someone who wasn't as educated as myself, unlikely to understand the books I read, the cultural references I made, or anything I did, I spent six months in the seclusion of my own home, occasionally taking my daughter to the playground, rejoicing in my growing belly and the kicks that came, tentatively, but they came.

My friends from the military quickly dispersed, as is the nature of military buddies—the relationship is, at best, transient. They were now in Germany, South Korea, North Carolina, and Kentucky.

So I spent those months alone.

Finding Common Ground

Was I in any way superior to them? No, but in my insecurity, and my fear of becoming a typical "teenaged mother," I wanted to think I was.

Eventually, towards the end of my pregnancy, I made friends. They didn't read as much or as often as I did, they had none of the educational aspirations I did, and they had never married, but were living with a boyfriend and children, invariably in convoluted stepchild/biological child arrangements.

But I saw myself in them.

They delighted in their children as much as I did in mine. They tried as best as they could to have natural childbirth, as I tried. They loved pushing their preschoolers on the swings, as I did. They expressed interest in what their older children did in school, they saved money for the hope of giving these children a better education, and they constantly reminded them to go out and make something of themselves, to chase their dreams, to try to be happy.

As I did.

A Recipe for Good Parenting

There is no age limit in parenting, and there is no certain age that you have to be before you can be a good parent. There is not, as I once preferred to believe, a minimum education level that you needed to attain, or a certain economic level, or anything else.

All that it takes to be a good parent, teenaged or otherwise, is to give freely of yourself, to love your child more than anything else in the world, and try to do your best, day by day.

Whether you're fourteen or forty, the same rules for being a good mother apply. I wish every mother in the world the best of luck, for it's the hardest job in the universe.

Being a Teenage Mom Helped Me Succeed

J. Anderson Coats

Nineteen-year-old J. Anderson Coats gave birth to a baby boy during her sophomore year at a state college. After taking a year off to raise her newborn son, she decided to re-enter college—at an elite all-women's school on the other side of the country.

At first, Coats found that selective colleges wouldn't look twice at a prospective student raising a small child. In her application and interview for her selected college, however, Coats found ways to shape her experiences as a young mother to her advantage. Along the way, she developed a genuine conviction that the challenges she had already faced—challenges foreign to most of her privileged classmates—had made her stronger, more capable, and more dedicated to her personal and academic success.

J. Anderson Coats graduated from Bryn Mawr College outside Philadelphia and also received a master's degree in library science. She continues to write about motherhood and related issues, and her essays have been published in several magazines and anthologies. She lives in the Pacific Northwest.

On Wednesday of spring break during my sophomore year of college, I gave birth to an eight-pound, three-ounce baby boy. I named him for a medieval Welsh prince and decorated the walls of his room in our tiny apartment with maps from the thrift store and handmade quilts.

I was nineteen years old.

The next Monday I was back in class, and for the next three months I ferried his little baby carrier back and forth to the university on the bus, in silent defiance of those who said my life was over. But by summer I had not registered for fall,

J. Anderson Coats, "Beyond the Ivy," *off our backs*, vol. 36, no. 1, January 2006, pp. 19–21. Copyright © 2006 off our backs, inc. Reproduced by permission.

and in September our little family moved across the country, three thousand miles from anyone I knew and anything familiar.

There I was, barely twenty with a six-month-old baby in a place where people drove too fast, spent too much and survived on a steady diet of cheesesteaks and a strange food called scrapple.

An Uncomfortable Start

I got us a small dark two-bedroom condo near a reservoir the realtor called a lake, but, speaking generously, it was a drainage ditch. Termites crawled up through the carpet, and when the landlord did nothing, I peeled the carpet back and sealed the termite-holes with toothpaste. I found grocery stores and playgrounds and took the baby for endless drives in search of a decent cup of coffee. In a few months I had my sea legs, and thought to finish my history degree at one of the many local colleges or universities.

But my new region did not offer the customary University of State Name I expected, and the local institutions had names that glowered down on me from on high—Penn, Temple, Princeton, Swarthmore. And none of them seemed particularly welcoming of a teen mother and state college dropout with empty pockets and a handful of pathetic transfer credits from some anonymous blip in the West.

These places were not for the likes of me.

A Long Shot

But whatever kept me waddling into Twentieth Century Art while nine months pregnant and barely able to fit behind the little desk made me send away for a packet from a Seven Sisters college and fill it out.

But while I filled out the application, I secretly wondered who I was kidding. This prestigious college wouldn't have a place for me any more than the other highbrow institutions. Places like these wanted the brilliant, the talented, the exceptional. I had been none of the above since high school, where I cracked 1300 on my SATs and graduated in the top one percent of my class. Where my pottery had been periodically on public display and I'd published several short stories in both local and national venues.

But that was more than two years ago, and no one would look at those things. Not while I had a diapered anchor clinging to my underage shoulder.

My grades from my prior university days were decent and several of my old professors were willing to supply good recommendations, but I hadn't spent my "year off" teaching kindergarten in a poor neighborhood or building a women's clinic out of mud and adobe in a third world nation. My grades and recommendations would speak for themselves, but somehow I had to bluff through the set of written questions accompanying the application, questions intended to gauge the applicant's level of recent accomplishment in the guise of a writing sample.

Real-Life Challenges

Think of a recent event or situation that challenged you. In what way did you confront the difficulties and what lesson did you learn?

"Over the summer, the politics of interpersonal relationships threatened the breakdown of a family superficially confident in its outward semblance of perfection. Certain biological difficulties presented me with the option of confrontation or negotiation; choosing the former, the lesson of difficulty's effect of separating gold from chaff will remain long in a fragile consciousness."

That is, parents don't want to become grandparents in their forties and they will let you know it. Siblings who ponder the baby's paternity and suggest abortion don't know how deeply it cuts. And friends whose eyes widen and who gradually drop from the radar aren't worth keeping, but those who keep calling will stay around forever.

What was the last book you read? How did it affect you?

"Oh, it was a fast-paced and gripping analysis of the politics of resistance and acceptance by means of unpacking the interaction of monochromatic femininity and the archetypal lupine viewed through the Utopian lens of the sublime Edenic greenwood."

That'd be "Little Red Riding Hood." Want to hear about prevailing notions of capitalism and deconstructionalism within the context of material selection in triumvirate porcine domestic architecture?

I sent in all the paperwork and stewed for months. I was convinced they wouldn't let me in. But I had written a damn good statement of purpose. I was out of my league. They didn't know that.

The baby learned to stand up and consumed his body weight in Cheerios.

A Different World

When the college called me for an admissions interview, I was elated. On my eighteenth birthday, my mother had rather optimistically bought me an interview suit and it still fit me the same as the day I tried it on. I looked like any other twenty-year-old prospective undergrad. I did not look like anyone's mother.

Before the interview, I had a tour of the campus. My student guide was a blonde-maned girl from upstate New York a year my junior who planned to major in chemistry. She chattered about clubs and parties and what dorm was the best to live in. I listened with a certain amount of patient irony, thinking how I hadn't even been to a movie since the baby's birth and wondering how my roommate would like tripping over gnawed board books while she put on her makeup for club-hopping.

The campus buildings were Gothic revival and magnificent with their weathered stone, roundel windows and pointed arches. A series of cobbled paths webbed through them. In-side, the original hundred-year-old woodwork shone beneath a mellow patina created from the sliding of endless hands. Three massive libraries housed almost a million volumes, including a substantial archives and rare books collection.

My guide flung a disinterested arm at the ornate Gothic structures with the casual air of one who never doubted she'd be at a place like this. For her, it had never been a worry. For her, it meant almost nothing.

The Interview

When we'd walked over the entire campus, she led me back to the cozy admissions building for my formal interview. The interviewer asked me what I planned to study, why I'd chosen that particular college and how I handled stress. My replies were cool and well-presented; history, because of the institution's proximity and academic strength in my discipline, and writing and long walks. I took a stroller on those walks and wrote during naptimes, but she didn't need to know that. She was smiling and nodding at my responses, and her demeanor told me I was doing well.

Finally, as we were standing up and saying goodbye, she happened to look at her notes and said, "I see you've taken a year off. What have you been doing? Working? Traveling?"

What went through my head was, "Oh yeah, right now my job is really grueling, seven days a week and no vacation time whatsoever. Five in the morning till eight at night, if I'm lucky, and it seems like every night I'm called in for the graveyard shift. The pay is lousy and there's no 401K, but the benefits are pretty nice."

But what came out of my mouth was, "No, I have a nine-month-old son and I've been staying at home with him."

The Big Question

She smiled and cooed and asked to see his picture. Then she dropped back into interviewer mode and asked, "Do you think having such a young child will affect your academic performance?"

What she meant was, "Do you really belong here? Shouldn't you be looking into hairdressing or medical transcription at community college?"

I did not hesitate or flinch. "Yes. He will affect my performance. For the better. I have a better reason to do well than some eighteen-year-old kid whose parents cut you a check once a year."

A Reason to Succeed

She leaned back, pursed her lips, then nodded. And it occurred to me, once I'd said it aloud, that not only would I do well, I'd do better than girls who did less all day than I did before nine in the morning, and I'd do it on half as much sleep.

Everything that had gotten me through that first grinding year of motherhood with its strung-out all-nighters, its isolation, its sidelong glances and mutters about my age—those were the very things that would see me through a prestigious Seven Sisters college and beyond. I would do well not despite being a teen mother three thousand miles in exile, but in a large part because of it. Because I had a damn good reach to do well and a lot more to lose if I didn't.

And success at an ivy-hung grey-stone place like this for me, underage with a baby on my hip and one box of pasta away from starvation, would mean more than it would to someone who expected it, who had never had to worry about her place in the world. Someone who had never had to make her own.

When my acceptance letter arrived several months later, I wasn't surprised. Only ready.

Parenting on a Dare

Amy Benfer

Amy Benfer gave birth to her daughter at the age of sixteen. In this essay, she writes as a thirty-year-old woman looking back on the biggest decision she had ever made: to become a teenage mother. She admits that at the time, both she and her parents realized that giving the baby up for adoption to a stable married couple would probably have been in the better interest of the child. But Benfer saw the situation as a dare, and wanted to prove that she could be a teenage parent and still achieve her dreams.

Benfer acknowledges that her parents' generosity enabled her to live as a normal teenager for the first two year of her daughter's life. But when it was time to go to college, Benfer broke away from the shelter of her parents' home to attend a school 3,000 miles away, and she never went back.

Benfer has made a career as a writer with her daughter by her side, and is now an editor for Salon.

My daughter was 4 days old on the day I decided to be her parent. My father was in the driver's seat. I was a 16-year-old leaking milk in the back seat of my parents' station wagon when I made the announcement: "Let's go get her."

"We're going to get the baby," my father said, and drove over a wall of traffic cones to cross over into the turn lane. And that was that: Me, my parents, my younger brother, all of us went on this reckless mission to pick up a newborn baby we'd left with my mother's single friend until we figured out what the hell to do with her. I don't know how my father got there without killing us all. We were all crying. We knew it

Amy Benfer, "Parenting on a Dare," Salon.com, May 10, 2003. This article first appeared in Salon.com at http://www.salon.com. An online version remains in the Salon archives. Reprinted by permission of the author.

was a stupid idea. We knew we could be seriously messing up at least two lives. We knew that there was a perfectly appropriate adoptive couple, of the right age and financial situation, with a mortgage, two cars and a nursery waiting for that baby. But somehow we all rushed into the friend's condo, claimed our baby, and took her home, where she went to sleep in a tiny crib that had housed my baby dolls not that many years before.

Making Promises

We all made promises to that child. My brother, who was 10 at the time, promised to donate all of his allowance for the next eight years, and a new pair of Bugle Boy jeans if we'd keep her. (We still haven't collected on that part of the deal, but I remind him every few years that coming through with at least the Bugle Boys is the right thing to do.) My parents promised to get me somehow to adulthood, by providing us both with a place to live and health insurance, giving me free childcare (from my stay-at-home mother) through high school and sending me on to college, as they had already planned to do.

My promise was the most complicated. On the morning my daughter was born, the doctor came in to talk to me. He knew my age. He knew there was an adoptive family waiting to take her (the bouquet they sent was on my nightstand). He knew I had not yet made the decision.

He told me that he was concerned with taking care of his patients' minds as well as their bodies. He said that, of course, the best decision for my daughter would be to place her for adoption. But, he said, perhaps I was not strong enough to make that choice.

My response? *F--- you.*

My doctor meant well, as did everyone else who had said more or less the same thing throughout my pregnancy. And I was the kind of girl that everyone believed would recognize that parenting my daughter as a teenager was not in the best interest of myself or my child.

But I took it as a dare. I had a 16-year-old's immortality complex. Up until then, nothing had been hard. I had had a safe, middle-class childhood in which the only dangers were those I got myself into—by, say, taking the family car in the middle of the night, or having sex.

I hated my doctor for implying, or so I thought, that keeping my child would be a sentimental decision made out of emotional weakness. To me, this was my chance to prove just how tough I was. Like most ambitious teenagers, I still believed at that time that I could choose between, you know, being president, winning the Pulitzer Prize for fiction (maybe poetry, maybe both) and maybe being a movie star or something in my youth. I was still going to do all that, and I was going to do it with a child. It was my chance to be extraordinary in the most literal sense, by breaking out of the ordinary college, career, dating, marriage, children trajectory that was expected of girls like me.

So my promise, to myself and my daughter, was that we were going to prove everyone wrong. I was going to raise a child who was every bit as smart, capable and badass as I thought I was. And I was going to do everything I would have done anyway, and do it just as well as, if not better than, I would have on my own. . . .

The Psychology of Teen Parenting

My mother and I, both of us big talkers, would have long, ponderous discussions on why, exactly, teenage mothers often did badly. We didn't know many of them at all, and none intimately. We came up with theories, some more crackpot than others. We took our cues from novels, from people around us, from pop psychology. Of course, there was the money thing and the education thing. But we wanted to understand the psychology of teen parenting. One of us—I'm not sure which one—came up with the idea that teenage mothers were often emotionally stunted at the age when they first became pregnant, because, as we decided, they hadn't "gone through all their developmental stages."

It was an arrogant pronouncement, one that certainly revealed that neither one of us had much experience with any situations that fell outside the range of typical family life, the kind of life we had just agreed that I was going to have.

I took it to mean that, at 16, I should act like a 16-year-old; at 18, like an 18-year-old; at 25, like a 25-year-old, and so on. The danger, as we saw it, was that if I gave up too much of my own identity into being a mother at a young age, I would resent my child and that would be a bad thing.

In other words, being a good mother, for me, was entirely dependent on how good I was at taking care of myself. I not only gave myself license to be selfish, but following my selfish instincts also became a moral imperative.

Being a Normal Girl

For the first two years of my daughter's life, my parents insulated me from the usual consequences of teenage motherhood. There was no question that I was my daughter's parent, but I certainly was not a single parent. My mother did the childcare from 8 AM to 3 PM; my father earned the income. My job was to do well in school and to enjoy my baby. And since my job was also to be a "normal" high school girl, I also went out with friends and to punk rock shows on the weekends after my daughter was asleep and to poetry club at the coffeehouse every two weeks. I was too busy to date much until the end of my senior year, but if I'd wanted to, I could have done that too.

Because it was so easy, I got bolder. The first major conflict between my parents' generosity and my own ambitions came around the time I started to apply to college. My parents, who had both gone to state schools, had once been perfectly happy to send me to whatever private school I wanted to attend. They still agreed that I should go to college, but they wanted to keep me close to home where they could help out. I saw no reason why I should scale back my ambitions just because I had a child. I applied to all the same schools I would have anyway and finally chose a very expensive school 3,000 miles away from home.

My parents were horrified, but in the end, they didn't stop me. I don't think anyone could have. When they said it was too expensive, I asked for their tax returns and suggested ways they could meet the expected parental contribution. When they worried about how we would live, I called the dean of my school and came back with childcare, a two-bedroom apartment, and a meal plan for us both. Two years later, when they told me they could not afford to pay for that school, I took a year off and went back as an independent student. My daughter and I moved to Connecticut when I was 18, and, except for brief visits back, I have never gone home again.

Every few years, I try to write an essay with the working title "Without You." It's supposed to be a piece that follows the imaginary person in my head, the version of myself who has lived a parallel life without taking that dare and deciding to raise a child at 16. I've never been able to write that story. Part of it must be that having a child shapes every part of a person's identity, so that it becomes impossible to imagine a self who has not been formed by taking care of that child. But the other reason I've never been able to write that story is that having a child didn't change me *enough*.

Fifteen Years Later

This year, I will have been a mother for exactly half my life. I'll turn 30 in less than a month; my daughter will turn 14 this summer. If you had asked me at 15 what I saw myself doing at 30, I would probably have said that I would be a writer living in New York. And, at 30, I live in Brooklyn and have made my living as a writer for nearly seven years. At 18, I was an English major at a college I loved. At 23, I moved to San Francisco to be near my boyfriend, a brilliant novelist whom I loved. At 25, I had my dream job as an editor at Salon (which, yes, I also love). And at 29, I moved to New York, where I am still doing work that I love. I'm not going to pretend that I couldn't write another version of my life about all the ways I've failed to get and do what I want. But it's difficult to believe that the bare outline of my life for the past 15 years would look any different if I'd had the freedom to construct it without taking my child into consideration.

I kept the first part of my promise to myself: Being a parent didn't stop me from doing what I wanted to do. The second part, is, of course, my promise to my daughter. Fifteen years after she was conceived, do I think I did right by her?

The worst part of being the parent of older children is that you see the effects of everything you have done. You know exactly how you have damaged your child, in the same way that you know exactly how your own parents have damaged you. It's a cost–benefit analysis. I don't always know what she thinks of me, but I know what kind of parent I am. I still have a nearly subhuman immunity to risk. After making the decision to raise a child at 16, few things compare. Nothing seems crazy to me. I am a warm parent. I love to talk to my daughter. But I'm also undisciplined. I'm messy. I'm selfish. We've never had enough money, enough space, enough time. When I fail—to clean the apartment, to meet a deadline, to find a job, to keep a lover—I have the same tendency to think f--- you. You try to raise a child on your own at 16 (at 22, 25, 29). It's an excuse. People let me use it more often than they should.

I am in the strange situation of having known the couple who wanted to raise my child if I had not chosen to do so. I selected them, I sat in their living room, I toured the house and talked with them about their philosophy of child-rearing.

We haven't spoken in 15 years, but I've heard enough to have an idea of where they are now. I know that in her parallel life, my child would have grown up the daughter of a social worker and a real estate agent in the Northwest. She would live in a four-bedroom house; she would have a summer cottage in the mountains. She would have been allowed to have a dog, and it's likely she'd have a brother and a sister. She wouldn't have seen as much of the world. She may have grown up to be more like the girl I was at her age, a suburban teenager longing for adventure and danger and a more exciting life. She would have been more stable.

I don't know that girl. She isn't my daughter.

The girl who is my daughter has been told her whole life that we almost didn't do it, that we almost lost our nerve. She knows as well as we do that was the sensible thing to do, and we haven't tried to hide it. As she's gotten older, she and I sometimes talk about what her life could have been like. She can't really imagine it, of course, any more than I can. I have an odd little line that I trot out sometimes. When she says she was an "accident," I tell her that she should feel that she is all the more a wanted child. We didn't want a child, I say, we wanted *you*. She wasn't convenient, she wasn't planned, she profoundly changed all of our lives. And we did it anyway.

I say "we" because I am thinking of the four of us in that station wagon, running over traffic cones on our way to do something that everyone else knew was a terrible idea. And you know what? We were exactly, exactly right.

SOCIAL ISSUES
FIRSTHAND

CHAPTER 3

Professionals Helping Teen Parents

Dealing with Teenage Pregnancy

Barbara J. Howard

Barbara J. Howard is a pediatrician who sees pregnant young women in her practice more often than she would like. In this article, which is written from the point of view of a pediatrician giving advice to other pediatric physicians, Dr. Howard describes her approach to working with pregnant teens.

Throughout her article, Dr. Howard stresses the importance of maintaining lines of communication—between a pregnant teen and her family and partner, between the patient and the doctor, and between the patient and other services available to her. Dr. Howard discusses the importance of defusing what could be a potentially tense situation in the doctor's office, and describes her own role as a compassionate, neutral advocate for her young patients.

Dr. Howard's article, in addition to providing some key statistics regarding teenage pregnancy and serving as a useful resource for other medical professionals, also provides insight into how doctors and other medical personnel think about and approach the complicated issues surrounding teenage pregnancy.

Dr. Barbara J. Howard is an assistant professor of pediatrics at Johns Hopkins University in Baltimore, Maryland. She is also the codirector of the Center for Promotion of Child Development Through Primary Care, a nonprofit organization that seeks to use the interaction between pediatricians and their patients and families to improve the overall condition of children's lives.

Teenage pregnancy is on the decline in our country, but it's still remarkably common, with 750,000 adolescents aged 15–19 years becoming pregnant each year.

Barbara J. Howard, "Dealing with Teenage Pregnancy," *Pediatric News*, Vol. 41, no. 6, June 2007, pp. 34–35. Copyright © 2007 International Medical News Group. Reproduced by permission.

Of course, we'd like to prevent those pregnancies that are unwanted, but the odds are not always on our side. A sexually active young woman who does not use contraception has a 90% chance of becoming pregnant in 1 year. And even though the majority of adolescents are waiting until they are a little older to have sex these days and using contraception when they do, contraceptive use is not consistent, reflecting adolescents' developmental sense of invulnerability.

A Guarded Reaction

When a teenager in my practice turns up pregnant, I have to be careful. My first reaction is often anger or disappointment, since I see prevention of teen pregnancy as an important part of my role as a pediatrician. Seeing a positive pregnancy test can make me feel like I've failed.

I work hard, though, to hide my personal reactions to a pregnant teen. It's about her, after all, not about me.

I have to recognize that the way I view teen pregnancy as a married, white, educated professional woman and physician may not reflect the cultural norms of young women in the community I serve, where teenage pregnancy may be the norm, and even a welcome sign of maturity, fertility, and independence. Some mothers expect to raise their daughters' first babies, just as their own mothers did when they became pregnant at 16. Rates of teen pregnancies are highly variable. In Baltimore, for example, half of first pregnancies are in mothers 19 and under. From a strictly biological point of view, this is a great age to bear children.

"Not Cause for Celebration"

In most cases, the news of a pregnancy is not cause for celebration in the pediatrician's office, and I like to be ready for what may be an emotional encounter. When a teenaged girl comes in and says, "I've been awfully tired lately," or presents with symptoms of a urinary tract infection, abdominal pain, breast tenderness, menstrual irregularity, or vaginal bleeding, it's a tip-off to me to make sure I get that patient alone as soon as I can. In many states, a sexually active teenager is a legally emancipated minor with the right to complete decision-making and confidential care. These rights are hard to provide if the teen's mother remains in the room as the possibility of pregnancy is broached and the telltale results of a pregnancy test arrive.

I think it's much better to share the news with the teenager alone, so I can ask her, "How are you going to talk to your parents about this?" If she is reluctant to tell her parents by herself, I offer to help her break the news with her in the room, or, if she requests, to tell the parents myself with her out of the room. Whether the teen is present or not, I try to shape the conversation to accept parental anger but move on quickly to teamwork. "Obviously, this is a big moment in your teen's life," I might say. "How would you like to come out of this in terms of her relationship with you?" I've had parents who scream at me and cry for half an hour before they can face their teenager calmly. Serving that role is OK with me. I want to make sure the teenager is safe and supported during this difficult time.

Note that I do not encourage the possibility that my patient will not confide the news to her parents, although each case is different. Sometimes when an adolescent says, "My parents are going to kill me," the potential for physical harm is real. In these rare instances, I do whatever I can to help her find resources independently.

In any case, it is the teen's decision whether and when to tell her family. Maintain confidentiality by being careful what you write on the diagnosis sheet if the bill is going to her parents. She may want to pay for the pregnancy test herself to avoid revealing the situation before she is ready.

A Compassionate Advocate

As pediatricians, we represent authority figures to teenagers. They may be afraid of our reactions, as well as those of their parents. I try to make it clear that I am here to be an advocate, offering objective but compassionate assistance for whatever decision she makes. I try to convey this through every pore of my being, and I do believe that if physicians are not comfortable being objective, they need to know ahead of time how to refer teens to someone who is. Planned Parenthood is an excellent resource—accessible in most communities—that provides adoption or abortion counseling and early prenatal care if she decides to keep the baby.

I always ask teenagers, "What do you think your partner is going to think of this pregnancy?" It's an important question for the answers it may reveal. Was this young woman having sex in an attempt to provide herself with self-esteem and comfort because she is depressed? Was she the victim of incest or date rape, or taken advantage of sexually in any way? How old is this partner? I get very concerned about coercive relationships if I hear that the partner is any more than 2–3 years older than she is.

Assess your patient's psychological well-being at this time, making sure she is not vulnerable to self-harm.

Exploring Options

Ask whether she has thought about what she is going to do. Some teens have thought about this in detail already and expected a positive test. Still, I think it is good to view the situation through the prism of the four domains of adolescent strengths and development outlined in "Bright Futures in Practice, Mental Health" (2002): belonging, independence, mastery, and generosity (www.brightfutures.org/mentalhealth). Keep in mind how the teen's behavior, strengths, and weaknesses fall into these categories. For example, you might explain that one young woman's drive to create an independent life and sense of belonging to a new family with her partner is actually appropriate for her age and that she has the generous qualities of a good mother. Also discuss the other skills she has mastered, evidenced by her good grades in school and college plans, and encourage her to consider how a choice of keeping this baby might influence these ambitions. Going through these domains will make it possible for teenagers to hear you, because you are touching on strengths they care about rather than telling them what to do.

Educate teenagers about their options, which include abortion, adoption, and keeping their babies. Statistics show that 57% of teens choose abortion, 29% give birth, and 14% miscarry. You should ensure that they have access to accurate information about each possibility, but keep in mind that you'll need to follow up, and follow up quickly.

The window for an abortion is narrow, and teens choosing to keep their babies need access to prenatal care as early as possible. I always specify that they should not drink, smoke, or use any drugs or medicines while they are deciding. I think this makes the responsibilities of pregnancy more real as well as beginning to protect the fetus.

I either schedule a follow-up appointment or call teens within a few days to see how they are doing with their decision, how they're doing with their families, and how I can help. Keep the door open to your young and vulnerable patients during this time, both for their well-being now and to promote thoughtful decisions later about their reproductive health.

Caught in the Middle

J.B. Orenstein

In this essay, emergency room physician J.B. Orenstein writes that "the healthiest-seeming patients are the ones I fear the most." Coming from a doctor who daily sees and treats the victims of the most awful injuries and illnesses, this statement is particularly striking.

Dr. Orenstein relates the story of a fifteen-year-old pregnant girl to illustrate his point. As he outlines his and his colleagues' attempts to counsel the girl and her family, he reveals the increasingly complicated situation into which he's drawn almost against his will. As events quickly spiral out of control, Dr. Orenstein vividly illustrates the complex, heartbreaking family dynamics that often accompany teen pregnancy. His story also shows his own attempts to strike a balance between professional distance and personal feeling.

Dr. J.B. Orenstein is a pediatric emergency room physician now practicing in Rockville, Maryland. His writing has appeared in the Washington Post *and* McSweeney's, *as well as in medical journals.*

When I introduce myself to people and reveal that I'm an E.R. [emergency room] doc, they get this excited little gleam in their eyes and ask one of two questions: "Is it tough?" or "How do you deal with the stress?"

I hate to disappoint the voyeuristically inclined, but the truth is, the tough, stressful part of the job has very little to do with plunging tubes down throats of unconscious people or yelling "Clear" and slamming defibrillator paddles. The hardest thing is to uncover the spiraling cascade of events, each one worse than the last, that sends a person to the E.R.

J.B. Orenstein, "Tales from the Emergency Room," Salon.com, April 24, 2000. This article first appeared in Salon.com at http://www.salon.com. An online version remains in the Salon archives. Reprinted with permission.

And that's why the healthiest-seeming patients are the ones I fear the most. For so often, they have the problems I'm simply not trained to fix.

A Bizarre Referral

Last month a colleague of mine working at an E.R. across town sent me a 15-year-old girl with a request to do an ultrasound to determine whether she was pregnant. I looked at her chart. Gulp. She had already been given a pregnancy test and the results were positive.

So why had my colleague deemed it necessary to order a wholly unnecessary test?

This was a board-certified E.R. doctor, an otherwise perfectly competent practitioner whom I had worked with for several years. While many doctors do have substance dependency problems, this guy was not on drugs. I called the doctor and he confessed: He was scared of facing the girl's mother.

The mom had made clear to him, in no uncertain terms, that her daughter was a good girl; her daughter didn't do that. We E.R. doctors like to think we're tough, that we can handle just about any hostile or obnoxious personality type. But he had caved.

He acknowledged that, yes, there were certain conditions that might result in a virgin's having a positive pregnancy test, but these were uniformly nasty: ovarian, pituitary or some other kind of hormonally active tumors. Rather than rule any of these out, he sent her over to the mother ship—to me—for an ultrasound.

Upon cross-examination as to the girl's presenting symptoms, he confessed that the mom had brought her to the urgent care center because she was vomiting and tired all the time. In other words, she was acting pregnant.

Just to be perfectly clear about it, this was the stupidest referral for a medical test in the annals of medicine. If she had been bleeding or complaining of crampy abdominal pain, and was in danger of miscarrying, she would, indeed, have needed an ultrasound. The procedure could have also found out if the girl was in any danger of having a tubal, or ectopic, pregnancy. But to do it to make sure that a pregnant girl is pregnant—well, that's lunacy.

Coming Up with Plan B

Once they arrived, I understood. This shameless act of cowardice by a doctor who knew better was fully excused by the fact that the mother was as big as a mastodon and wore the demeanor of an irritable boar. She bullied her way past the triage nurse and planted herself in the middle of the E.R., loudly demanding the whereabouts of Dr. Orenstein. Her daughters (a younger sibling was also in tow) cowered in terror behind her.

My initial plan—to extricate myself by telling her that her daughter was with child and to check in with the OB-GYN clinic—was not going to do. So, in what was arguably one of the most wasteful moves in my career, I sent the daughter for the ultrasound. I figured it would give me time to formulate a Plan B, not to mention devise retribution against my colleague for sending me this mess.

By the time she arrived at our hospital, the girl was thoroughly distraught. At least the sonogram would give her time away from her mother. With her I sent our social worker, a wonderfully sensitive, empathetic human being who could cajole a confession out of [mobster] John Gotti. But she was powerless to get the girl to own up.

"Don't Tell Mom"

My shift is only 12 hours long. I checked my watch. If I could somehow stall the girl in the ultrasound room for another, oh, nine hours, then I could palm her off onto someone else. As I deliberated how I would actually go about doing this, the girl was wheeled back with her sister, accompanied by the only report possible from the sonographer: normal, intrauterine pregnancy.

Plus, three words from the girl: Don't tell Mom.

Now it was my turn to do something eminently dumb. The only problem was, I didn't know which dumb option to pick: Respect the girl's wishes and leave her to figure out how to deal with her pregnancy, or sweet-talk her into letting me tell Mom and thereby preclude any chance of her ever getting an abortion—which, according to the social worker, was what the girl wanted and what the mother would never approve.

Fortunately, the social worker provided me with a third way out. I would call in the authorities on the case. The girl had the right, as an emancipated minor, to make her own reproductive decisions. If, however, the boyfriend turned out to be older than 18, she was also a rape victim and we had the onus to report it. If not, we might not have to call in the child welfare workers.

Breaking the News

I played bad cop, the social worker played good cop, but we were both cops: Tell us the truth and we won't say a word to your mother. Coercion. The social worker had her pegged better than I did. She bet the girl would sooner face her mother's wrath than give up the boyfriend. I bet she would jump at the chance to get an abortion by giving up the father and eluding her mother.

She clammed up about the baby's father and broke the truth to her mother. Mom exploded into torrents of maternal despair. She wailed, shrieked, sobbed, threatened, beat at her mammoth breast and finally swore on her grandmother's grave that her daughter would never leave her sight again. She would personally raise her grandchild until her own daughter became a fit mother.

When the social worker and I explained that she didn't have the right to make that decision for her daughter, she dared us to do anything about it. Talk about scary. Here was a

275-pound hailstorm of fury daring us to interfere in her family dynamics, and all we had for protection was a scrawny security guard 50 yards away.

An Ugly Truth

The social worker held her ground, firmly repeating that if the girl's boyfriend was older than 18, she was legally in the purview of child protective authorities. Barely audible, the girl miserably admitted to a 15-year-old boyfriend who had returned to their country in Central America. The sister nodded briskly at the revelation, as if unburdening herself of a long-held secret. The social worker and I still gamely played out our hand, but it was over. The girl had the right to choose what she would do with her womb, but she was no match for her betrayed, towering mom.

The social worker went to the authorities anyway—to nominally check on the girl's story but also to give her a fighting chance. The girl wanted an abortion, and at eight weeks pregnant, she had only four weeks left before she would be too far along.

The investigators very quickly found out what, I believe, the social worker had already guessed: The "boyfriend" was no pimple-bound adolescent but her own father. We were not, it turned out, the first ones to coerce her to give up some hidden part of herself.

It explained a lot: not only why she couldn't reveal the true father, even at the risk of incurring her mother's wrath, but also why her mother had so ferociously denied her pregnancy. On some level, she must have known.

A Court Appearance

With that information, the case was brought before a local magistrate. The child protection workers recognized the girl's desire for an abortion but also listened to the mother's case. She obviously cared for her daughter a great deal, was adamantly opposed to an abortion on religious and personal grounds and would be a willing and loving godmother for the baby. The judge, in full possession of the facts, and presumably in full possession of his faculties, ruled that a mother knows what's best for her daughter. (Or maybe he, too, was afraid of the mother.)

The girl was now at 10 or 11 weeks and within a week would be beyond hope of an abortion. Her appointed attorney filed an appeal and the social worker testified on the girl's behalf.

In a rare act of courage, I offered to appear in court as well. E.R. doctors spend an average of eight to 12 minutes with a patient and then move on to the next case. We jump in and out of people's lives; we don't jump back in. The demands of negotiating an acute injury or sudden illness create a thick, tough skin, but come at us the wrong way and we're only as tough as eggshell. The same eight to 12 minutes spent consoling a family or sharing in their mourning is beyond the ability of most of us. It takes a certain cowardice to intervene in someone's life—offering lifelong consequences good or ill—and then not face the family.

No Easy Cures

I never needed to appear. A few days after the filing, the deed was done. The court of appeals judge expedited a review and quickly sided with the girl. I imagined her being whisked away, alone, to a secret clinic for an intimate procedure, and then it was over.

Dad vanished; the girl disappeared into the custody of a foster family. Reduced to a husk by losses she'd never comprehend, the imposing mother went home to raise her remaining daughter.

So sometimes it's the patients who have nothing wrong with them who are the worst off of all. Given the terrible pathology lurking behind it, the girl needed her pregnancy terminated, and the family that allowed the sin needed help. But there were far better places to go to have the situation treated. The E.R. has no cure for a broken family, but in this case, as in so many others, it was where the family ended up. Our door was open and in they came.

A Path to Activism

Benita Miller Johnston

Benita Miller Johnston is an advocate for young mothers. She is the founder and director of the Brooklyn Young Mothers' Collective (formerly the Brooklyn Childcare Collective), a nonprofit organization whose mission is "to break the cycle of generational poverty among pregnant and parenting low-income mothers by helping them actively engage in improving the conditions that impact their lives." By providing education and support and training the next generation of women leaders, Johnston is helping to improve the lives of young women and children in New York City and beyond.

A lawyer by training, Johnston here outlines the roots of her advocacy work not only in her early work with the Legal Aid Society, but also in her personal and family history. Herself the daughter of teenage parents, Johnston seeks to give the young women she works with the same kinds of support and opportunities that were more available in previous decades. In addition, as the mother of young children, Johnston feels a sense of kinship with her young clients, a sense of common purpose and mutual support that enables her to see these girls as individuals and to respect the work they do.

I stay up late most nights thinking about the girls that I work with. I wonder whether they rub their bellies and hum quiet prayers meant for God to hear and answer. I did these things when I carried my babies. I marveled as my belly wriggled into humps and moved toward my touch. My babies and I knew each other well before we made our in-person acquaintance!

I wonder whether the girls that I work with worry about whether they will have enough. Enough love to keep them happy; enough energy to keep them going; enough time to get the things they want.

I worry, I worry and then I worry some more.

Imagining the Past

I look at their smiling brown faces and imagine my mother. Like them, she once wedged a protruding belly into a desk meant for teen girls that scrawled the football star's name on their sneakers and had no reason to worry about hard-bottom shoes. She was 16 in 1969 when she gave birth to my brother, and I quickly followed 13 months later. Today, I tease her, reminding her that I'm that dreaded and pesky too-soon subsequent birth. My mother is far removed from the day when she was pushed out of school and into a marriage that, in the last 36 years, has resulted in four children and nine grandchildren. Nowadays, she's a registered nurse. I look at my girls tangling their arms around young boys on the brink of fatherhood—nervous, sly smiles turning up the corners of their mouths when they greet one another. They have so much work to do. These boys' lives will not be like my father's as there are no auto factories brimming with jobs paying a wage high enough to head a household. But, they see me and know that for my girls I want what my mother got from my father, my grandmothers and our extended community. She had love, support and guidance.

Making a Difference

Two years ago, I started the Brooklyn Childcare Collective to provide legal information and social services support to pregnant and parenting girls after working as an attorney at Legal Aid Society. I mostly enjoyed the experience of trying to use my law degree to positively affect the lives of children, but as I grew older, I watched the parents flowing into the courthouse to answer criminal charges appear younger. Mostly, they were black and brown girls with their mothers, other female relatives or friends. Being nudged toward the table where decisions would be made about their family's life, they always tried to figure me out—bewildered, afraid and very much in love with their children, they often thought that the law guardian was the person that literally took their children in. Explaining my role often added another confusing layer of disruption to their lives. I wanted to be something different in relationship to them, not just be their child's attorney. I broke rules. Did things lawyers aren't supposed to do. I held hands with these young mothers, listened to them, gave comforting smiles and encouraged them in their mothering.

I knew that I had to move on so I started the Collective, believing that I could use the best tools I learned in the courtroom and wed them to my organizing experiences to create a dynamic community-based program. I started small with my own child strapped to my chest. I talked things up in Brooklyn Family Court and in the schools, and then was given an opportunity to launch a school-based program. The young mothers that I met at Brooklyn's P932K, helped me deepen my vision and together we questioned everything. Through questioning we are making personal and environmental changes. We are doing work in our schools, we are working in the courthouse, we birth in ways that honor our personal choices and ancestors. We are rearing our children in a woman-centered circle. We hold our babies to our breasts. We do our homework. We share our love in a way that affirms our dignity. We celebrate multiethnic and intergenerational friendships. We search for ways to get enough.

Finding Support

As young mothers on the verge, juggling school and good, safe childcare is a major challenge. While the New York City Department of Education provides childcare placements for student parents, often these slots are not convenient or situated in a good educational setting. Moreover, young mothers often report that because there are so few slots, many quickly fill up. We struggle around this issue of trying to create enough slots because we know that childcare is a critical component to ensuring that these young women have the time and mental energy needed to explore their own academic and personal possibilities.

While we expect the school system and local government to respond to the needs of young mothers, we also seek out the support and guidance of our elders. We know that healthy mothering never happens in isolation. We consciously develop relationships that broaden our understanding of our experiences as women. We never can get enough of these types of relationships and as young mothers these relationships are critical, especially when we talk about baby-making. When a 13-year-old mother in foster care asked me to define ovulation, I needed to connect to women more knowledgeable. When two 17-year-old expectant mothers said with a level of authority that shocked me that if you jump up and down following intercourse you can get all of the sperm out of your body and prevent pregnancy, we huddled around a blackboard and quickly did our best to dispel this myth. Outside of the rudiments of academia, my girls need knowledge that will literally save their lives. One can never get enough of these types of connections.

The Power of Love

I've learned not to underestimate the power of their love. Love for their children. Love for the partners. Love for themselves and each other. Often, the force of this love is lost to anger, frustration, envy and lack of understanding. We make an effort to strengthen these bonds for the benefit of the babies and for the sustenance of the girls. They need to be touched, they need smiles, and they need to be told that they are amazing. I tell them these things. I touch them. I know that this telling and touching matters because over time I see them do it with each other.

Last Sunday, my baby girl burned with fever and we were stuck indoors. I stared out of the window at Brooklyn (my adopted home, I'm a Detroiter) and listened to the cold wind whip against the concrete. I felt alone. I had work piled on my desk but it went untouched. Instead while cradling my daughter I was deep in thought about my girls. I thought about those waiting for babies to arrive. I thought about those struggling through math problems, fighting with boyfriends, or simply feeling overwhelmed. I wanted them in my living room with me. I wanted to talk and share. I wanted to listen to them plan their lives. I needed to connect to someone that would understand my yearning and I reached out to a sister/mentor in Detroit. She's been doing this work as a school principal for quite a while. I wanted her to tell me that I was right and that the work I had chosen was worthwhile. Even before I asked, she moored me, told me stories—reminded me that this is my life's work.

Fighting for Equal Access to Education

Katherine Arnoldi

As a young woman—and a young mother—Katherine Arnoldi could never quite accept the idea that life is unfair. She has spent the last thirty years working to make life more fair for other young mothers, particularly by advocating for easier, more affordable access to higher education.

In this article, Arnoldi traces her journey to activism, pointing out that her struggle has taken many forms, from setting up booths and distributing information to counseling individual mothers to taking legal action. Arnoldi's primary goal is to keep teenage mothers in high school and then educate them about how to put college within their financial reach. She also encourages higher education institutions to make college and university life more feasible for single mothers.

In 1998 Arnoldi wrote and illustrated the graphic novel The Amazing True Story of a Teenage Single Mom *about her own experience trying to attend college. More recently, she published a collection of short stories as well as the online Guide to Colleges for Mothers. She also has sponsored a scholarship fund for teenage moms. Arnoldi continues to advocate, both in person and on the Internet, for fair and equal access to education for young mothers.*

"What's this about fair," my mother would say, pulling my brother and I out of a life-threatening brawl. "The world is not fair." My mother should know. She was a single mom with three kids to raise in the 60s. She was about as angry as a person could be about unfairness. She was a perpetual time bomb of high blood pressure and bitterness.

Katherine Arnoldi, "Fair Means Fair," *The Mothers Movement Online*, December 2005. http://www.mothersmovement.org/features. Reproduced by permission.

I was never able to accept an unfair world, either. First, of course, my mother was unfair, but before I knew it I was a teen mom and about to see just how unfair the rest of the world could be, too. Working in a factory gave me even more fodder for my arsenal of injustice, and I held on tight to my belief that the world should be fair and I wanted to do everything I could to make it that way. After all, I had my daughter to consider.

First I had to learn to fight for equal access to education. For that story see the graphic novel *The Amazing True Story of a Teenage Single Mom* (Hyperion, 1998), the story of how I found Jackie, another single mom with two kids who said the two words that changed my life forever: *financial aid*.

Speaking from the Margins

Jackie made me see that single moms did not have equal rights in four ways: to fairness in the courts, to employment, to housing and to education. I wanted the world to be fair and I wanted to do my part. But how could a single mom who had a long way to go to work up to subsistence living help anyone else? Who would ever listen to me? I had a sneaking suspicion that if I ever mentioned these things people labeled me as crazy, which I realized everyone had done toward my mother. Once marginalized, it feels like you are yelling out on an empty plain.

In 1976 I wrote my first article for single moms about buying property with owner financing for a magazine called *Hard Labor*. I had this idea I had garnered from structural materialist anthropologists that those in power had the money and if single moms could own property, the basis of wealth I thought, then we would have more power. I also realized that I was one of only two single moms on campus at the University of Arkansas and that something was wrong with that, which made me mad and furious that I, for example, had waited two years on the waiting list for "married student" housing which was a dark concrete hell with not a tree or blade of grass in sight in the shadow of the gargantuan, luxurious football stadium where thousands of red-clad Razorbacks yelling "Pig Souie" disturbed my few minutes of precious study time. I knew there were plenty of single moms in the town and plenty in the state, the second poorest state in the country. I also surmised that when a sorority girl became pregnant she had to disappear, her education over, or else would return a year later with a new baby sister in the family.

A Bill of Rights

Jackie, meanwhile, was in North Carolina visiting teen moms in her poor rural county bringing them the hope of going back for their GED [general equivalency diploma] and eventually college. As I pursued a master's in literature in North Carolina and then creative writing in New York City (where I moved because I wanted to publish a book about teen moms), I, too, took financial aid forms and college applications to GED programs, realizing that if teen moms were coerced to leave high schools, as they are, then go and valiantly get their GED, they miss out on guidance counseling and information about financial aid and college.

What threw me over the edge of anger was seeing a photo in the *New York Times* in 1987 of a teen mom with a baby in one arm and a teddy bear in the other, a trivialization of the immensity of that young girl's problem. The article was about the epidemic of teen pregnancy and I could see it all coming then, how teen moms would be blamed for the economic crises caused by the Savings & Loan bailout and Desert Storm, all the way up to the End Welfare as We Know It frenzy. It's not FAIR, I yelled, just as I had at my mother about my brother.

I wrote up a lengthy tome, the Single Mother's Bill of Rights, which [editor] Pat Gowans published in the *Welfare Mother's Voice*, along with my other articles about unfairness and justice.... I had been publishing my rants on the subject in *The Quarterly* ..., *Room of One's Own* and *Blue Collar Review* but I also started, inspired by the East Village cartoonists in my neighborhood ... to make my own cartoon book. I thought that if I gave out the story of my life to the teen moms I was seeing in the GED programs, then they would understand that I, too, had many of the problems they had. I xeroxed it myself, adding to it each time before I would spend all night at the 24-hour copy center, along with all the other anarchists of the East Village, self-publishing our manifestos.

Reaching Out

I wanted a home for my "operations" and I approached Armando Perez and Chino Garcia at the Charas Community Center two blocks from where I was living—on 9th Street between B and C—and eventually I started the Single Mom College Program there in the early 90s. Every Saturday I sat outside at a table and handed out financial aid forms and gave out college advice, most especially trying to entice moms by the amount of Pell Grant available a year, $4,000; SEOG [Supplemental Educational Opportunity Grant], $4,000; TAP state tuition assistance, $3,000, and advising on how to avoid loans. I went with the revolutionary Charas folks as we set up booths at street fairs and festivals in Tompkins Square Park.

I went to the Blue Mountain Center, a socially conscious art center and there, Harriet Barlow, Ben Shrader and Jonathan Rowe of Redefining Progress inspired me that my little zine should be published. The next year it won a New York Foundation of the Arts Award in Drawing and that inspired me to give it to my agent, Jennifer Hangen, and so *The Amazing True Story of a Teenage Single Mom* was published and I was suddenly on the *Today Show*, Tom Brokow and the Nightly News, CNN Entertainment and NPR getting to say that teen mothers do not have equal access to education, and if they are raising almost half of our country's children could not this lack of equal rights contribute to the feminization of poverty? I also was able to say that there appears to be a societal shift from nuclear family to single parenting and, just like the shift from extended family to nuclear family, it is women and children who are suffering. We need to lift the institutions up to our level of responsibility, I said.

Taking (Legal) Action

And just in case the institutions did not want to do so on their own, I started a class-action lawsuit against the New York City Board of Education with the New York Civil Liberties Union for coercing teen moms to leave high school. Enid Mastrianni, formerly of the Upstate Welfare Warriors, and I started looking at the top 300 colleges for accessibility for moms. The results were dismal. The idea is to use Title IX, which guarantees gender equity in education (nothing in it about sports, by the way) to get the colleges to provide equal accommodations for mothers, since having children is a gender characteristic. A long shot, but, as I am still fueled by anger, I think it's worth a try.

My anger has not subsided, especially as I now find that the incidence of single parenting is going up the world over, now 30 percent in Mexico, and up to 17 percent in Malaysia, and growing. Thanks to the World Bank and the WTO [World Trade Organization] and their neoliberal agenda, countries are doing what our country had done over the past twenty years: sign welfare bills, cut spending on education, health and social welfare, provide a military for global riot control and to protect the interests of the World Bank, and women who have been living a subsistence living are seeing their fields being taken over to grow exportable crops such as coffee and other unedibles and are forced to migrate to the cities, where, voila!, they are needed for the factories to make more exports out of plastic and other distressingly meaningless compounds. That's why my next graphic novel is about how women have been affected the world over by the neoliberal agenda. The fight for justice is just beginning and I am grateful to have been and to be a part!!

From Hopelessness to Inspiration

Rita Naranjo

Rita Naranjo has certainly traveled through adversity to get where she is today. Growing up in an unstable family situation, traveling from foster home to foster home before being reunited with her unpredictable, drug-addicted mother, Naranjo found herself sinking into the same kind of violent, hopeless, self-destructive lifestyle that had ruined her own mother's life. Engaged in theft and drug dealing, Naranjo got pregnant after a one-time affair that was a desperate cry for affection.

Despite pressure from authorities to terminate her pregnancy, Naranjo insisted on keeping her daughter. Her determination to stand up for her desires was just the start of a long, difficult journey to ensure that her daughter would have a safer, happier, more secure childhood than Naranjo herself did. Originally focused primarily on financial independence and security, Naranjo eventually discovered the additional rewards of speaking out about her own experiences and helping others in similar circumstances.

Rita Naranjo has been involved in many organizations devoted to helping youth, particularly current and former foster children, in California. She has received awards and other recognition for her advocacy work. Naranjo graduated from San Diego State University in 2004 and is currently pursuing a master's degree in social work with a goal of bringing about positive change in the foster care system.

I have had many days when I felt so hopeless that it was difficult to lift my head to look up at someone.

Rita Naranjo, "From Hopelessness to Inspiration," *You Look Too Young to Be a Mom*, New York: Perigee, 2004, pp. 242–250. Copyright © 2004 by Deborah Davis. Used by permission of Penguin Group (USA) Inc., and Deborah Davis (UK).

I was taken away from my mother when I was four years old. Over a ten-year period, I lived in a series of foster homes. I grew up with overwhelming sadness, hurt, mind-boggling confusion. For a long time I didn't understand why I'd been taken away from my mom. I spent many nights crying and crying, hiding my anguish from the people around me. Nobody ever gave me a hug and explained what was going on or that someday things would get better.

At age thirteen, I got arrested for possession of crack cocaine with the attempt to sell. When the cops got me, I had over four hundred dollars on me. I was put on house arrest and I was checked up on a couple of times a day. At this time I was back with my mother, only because I kept running away from my group home placements. I was so tired of being moved around from place to place. All I wanted was to be with my brothers, or at least see them more than twice a month. I hated my mother. I figured that if she loved my brothers and me she would stop using drugs and do what she had to do to get us back. Her attempts always failed; she broke all her promises. My mother could not tell me she loved me without me shouting back at her, "*You are a liar!*"

Running Out of Hope

By the time I turned fourteen I felt as though I had exhausted all sense of hope. I was back with my mother and brothers, but she continued to be heavily addicted to drugs and had no control over me. I was in high school, but I never went. *Why should I?* I thought, *nobody cares whether I go to school or not.* I spent as little time as possible at home, because I could not stand to see my mom in her drugged-out condition. The image of her being high had always haunted my dreams while I was younger, and it was now a frontline reality. I saw my mother smoke crack and drink and then become completely incoherent. It hurt me deeply to see her that way.

That year my mom, my six-month-old twin brothers, my ten-year-old brother, my thirteen-year-old brother, and I were evicted from our apartment. One brother who had gotten in trouble was put back into foster care. The rest of us were on the street with nowhere to go, and we had lost almost everything from the apartment. We were able to pack only one or two small suitcases and whatever could fit in a tiny car along with six people.

I was still on probation. When my probation officer came to check on me and I wasn't home, he put out a warrant for my arrest.

Being homeless did not impede my mother's ability to obtain and use drugs. Nothing else seemed to matter to her. We tried staying with some of my friends, but our stays were brief; people did not want my mom at their house.

Becoming a Survivor

Eventually my mom was arrested, and Child Protective Services picked up three of my little brothers. I could not believe that my family was falling apart again! I was scared, but I was mostly in shock. What gave me comfort and confidence was that I knew how to survive on the streets. I had friends that I hung out with—my "crew," my "road-dogs." We could burglarize any house, steal almost any car, sell any drug, and even rob people. I was good at planning, strategizing, and carrying out all these illegal acts. I felt like people owed me. I did not feel bad at the time because I knew the rich people I stole from would be able to buy more things. I was not concerned with material things. I was robbing and stealing to survive. I just wanted the bare necessities, food and shelter.

My mom was in jail for three months, for being under the influence and for child endangerment. All this time I gained and maintained much respect from my friends; they knew my situation and saw me as a survivor. I was the only female around most of the time, but growing up as a major tomboy,

I was tough and demanded respect. Though I was not known for being some easy female, some guys are very persistent and will not quit until they get what they want. And that is what happened. One of my so-called friends kept pressuring me to have sex with him. I was hesitant because the year before, when I was thirteen and had run away from a group home along with some other girls, I had gotten drunk and then was raped. I was very unwilling to have sex after that. Nevertheless, I eventually agreed to have sex with him, in part because I thought that maybe he really liked me. Those were truly false hopes. Believe me when I say it was not enjoyable. It was literally a *wham, bam, thank you, little girl* experience. He went to jail two days later for having a sawed-off shotgun, and he remained there for a long period of time due to repeated probation violations.

No Second Chance

While my mom was in jail, I was convinced that how I was living was probably how I'd live for the rest of my life. When she got out she came looking for me. She knew where my stomping grounds were, so it wasn't hard to find me. She arrived in a van with the attorney who represented her. I stood there cursing them both out and telling them to get the hell away from me. I did not want to give my mother another chance. I did not want to fall for another false promise. I told them I would rather stay on the street than go home. I was also afraid that her attorney was going to turn me in, since there was still a warrant out for my arrest.

Mom and the attorney eventually drove off without me. As angry and resentful as I was, in the back of my mind I knew I should go back home. I had a strong feeling that I could be pregnant. I was not sick at all and had never really kept track of my monthly cycle, so I am not quite sure how I knew. When my mom came to find me again, I went with her,

half-relieved and half-resentful. As usual, she acted like everything was okay, like nothing traumatic had happened to her
children.

Pregnant and Incarcerated

When I found out I was pregnant, I could have screamed and
cried and thrown up all at the same time. I lay in bed that
night in the dark, wide awake, and began to cry. I could not
believe that I was going to have a child. I felt that I had taken
a hopeless turn. How could I be a mother? What did I have to
offer?

I turned myself in to the juvenile court system to take care
of the warrant that was out for my arrest. I did not want to
get arrested while I was big and pregnant or after I had my
child, because they might try to take her away from me. I was
not going to let that happen. The court set a date for me to
"surrender," and the authorities ended up taking me into custody, pregnant and all. They didn't ask how my life was going
outside the courtroom, and I was not about to tell them.

In Juvenile Hall I received prenatal care. At my first
doctor's appointment they spent a lot of time talking about
the option of ending the pregnancy. They gave me booklets
and information brochures about abortion—right after they
had let me hear the baby's heartbeat. I left there feeling completely lonely and ashamed. They had treated me like a child
who had absolutely no potential whatsoever to provide anything positive to another child. They may have had good reason to believe that, but I was determined to prove them and
everybody else wrong. No way was I going to kill my baby.

More Closed Doors

I went right away to enroll back in school. The local public
school officials did not think it was a good idea for me to attend their schools while pregnant—another form of rejection.
I refused to let them discourage me. They had referred me to

Ocean Shores High, a continuation school with a teen parent program and on-site child care. I headed straight there. My first impression was very positive, and I looked forward to going to school—a completely new experience for me.

All my education up to this point had been very unstable and of poor quality. I felt completely ignorant in math and had much difficulty with writing. I must have been at a low grade level, because in the beginning it was hard for me to do the work successfully. Somehow, my self-confidence kept me going even when things seemed too difficult.

"A Whole New Person"

February 17, 1995, was a very painful but joyous day for me: the day that my daughter Sativa was born. I had been having pains since early in the afternoon the day before. Around 10 PM I knew it was time for me to head to the hospital. We did not have a car, and the hospital was about a mile away. I did not call the ambulance, because we would not have been able to pay the bill. The only alternative was to walk. My mom walked with me to the hospital late that night. Labor lasted for a really long time, and I thought that I was going to die. I forgot all that when I saw my precious little girl.

Soon after I had Sativa I returned to school. I was a whole new person, more focused and determined. My home life continued to be hectic and unhealthy, but school was my safe haven, a place of serenity that surrounded me with encouragement and support. For the first time in my life, people actually had something positive to say to me. They told me how smart I was. They told me I had the ability to pursue my dreams.

Driven to Succeed

I focused on finishing high school so that I could move on to higher education. I knew that was what I needed to do to make it in life. I did not want to be poor and worry about how to put food on the table, and even though part of me did not believe that I could succeed, I forced myself to keep trying anyway. Nobody else was going to be there to take care of my daughter and me. Sativa's father was out of the picture, and I refused to be dependent on any man.

At times I was at my wits' end and wanted desperately to leave the craziness at home, but I would have violated my probation if I'd left. Searching for a legal way out, I went to my probation officer and asked if I could legally emancipate. She told me I had two choices: to go back to Juvenile Hall or to go back into foster care. Either way, she said, I'd probably lose custody of my daughter. I stayed at home. I was not going to let it drive me insane. I kept my mind and heart focused on school and my daughter.

Leaving Home

When I was sixteen I went to my court review hearing. The judge was so impressed with my progress in school and in life, he said, "I don't see any reason for you to continue on probation; therefore, your case is officially being closed." I wanted to jump straight up out of my chair with excitement, but I figured I should maintain my composure just in case the judge decided to change his mind.

As soon as I got home, I acted on impulse: I packed my bags and left. Life at home was unsafe. My mom was recovering and going through withdrawals and because of that was always violent and angry. I was so determined to get out that I did not give a lot of thought to where I would go. My daughter's father was out of jail now, and I ended up with him and his family, but life at their house was not any better. Everyone was doing drugs and getting high, and I could not stand it. I moved from one place to another, but was continuously surrounded by drugs. Eventually my daughter's father and I cleared a bunch of crackheads out of an abandoned house that was undergoing foreclosure and moved in. I got the utilities turned on. During this time I was selling marijuana to make ends meet, but I did not want to engage in any more illegal activity; the thought of losing my daughter terrified me. After much deliberation I applied for public assistance. I hated the thought of having to do this. Not only was I a "teen mother" and a "former foster child," but now I was about to add another negative label—"welfare mother." I humbled myself and did what was necessary.

Getting Ahead

I thought my life would never see stability; nevertheless, I kept on going to school. I spent hours on the bus with Sativa or pushing her stroller to and from school. Many days I wanted to cry from exhaustion and discouragement, and some days I had to talk myself out of giving up, but I was also thankful that I was able to take Sativa with me to school, where I knew she was in a safe and healthy environment.

When I was still sixteen, I started taking classes at the local community college. I had heard from my counselor at school that I could take those classes and get college and high school credit simultaneously. I thought this was a great opportunity for me to get ahead, and it enabled me to graduate early from high school, I graduated when I was seventeen with a GPA of 3.67. People at school asked me to give the commencement speech at graduation. The local newspaper interviewed me, and the article appeared on the front page of the local section on graduation day. My spirits were higher than they had been in my entire life.

Safe at Last

Now I wanted to get out of the abandoned house and away from my daughter's dad. I felt he was holding me back and was not willing to change his lifestyle. Plus, I was not emotionally attached to him. We had stayed together up to this point because we had a child together. Just a few days after I had started looking for an apartment, I came home from school to find my windows and door boarded up. I think God decided to bless me once more, because I met an older couple who let me rent their cute one-bedroom rental house only five minutes from the beach. They even gave me the key before I had the entire first month's rent paid.

I was seventeen when I moved in. I finally felt a sense of security. No more drugs and violence. At last, it was just my daughter Sativa and me.

Starting to Make a Difference

By now I was a full-time student at MiraCosta Community College. I had child care and a stable home. A few of my brothers and their friends found my living room floor to be a place of comfort. I was fully independent except for the assistance I was receiving from the state, but I used that to my full advantage. I got a campus job doing outreach and recruitment at one of the local high schools and I loved it. I was making a difference. Even though I planned to major in business, I still wanted to help people.

One day, a really nice woman came to my house to bring my brother a basketful of household supplies. She told us about a project that she had started called the Former Foster Speakers Panel. She explained that participants talked to foster parents and social workers about their foster care experience, offering their insight and understanding. My brother Gino and I agreed to get involved.

Speaking Out, Setting Goals

I was completely overjoyed with the response to my first speaking engagement. People lined up to tell me how inspiring my story was and how much I had impacted them. I liked the feeling it gave me and was interested in making it last. That started my community activism, and the more I spoke, the more it changed my outlook on life. Before, my main interest had been to make money for my future and spend some time helping others. But one day as I sat outside the conference room where I had just spoken on a panel in front of hundreds of people, I decided to get my degree in social work. I wanted to be an activist and change the system.

Because of my speaking engagements, my reputation and network began to grow. People wanted me to speak at fund-raising events, at teen mother graduations, and at many other gatherings. In the meantime, I was moving further along in school and had more to talk about. In the year 2000 I graduated from MiraCosta Community College and I gave birth to my beautiful son, Amir. Before that, of course, I met the perfect man. Right after graduation I transferred to San Diego State University.

Everything that I have gone through—both good and bad—has had an impact on my ability to make a difference. I still have much to learn, but I already have a lot to offer. I want to be the mother that I never had. I want to be a friend to a foster child, the friend I'd always wanted when I was younger. I want to complete and succeed in higher education when nobody else in my family has. I want to make changes where nobody thinks change can happen. I know I want a lot of things, but I believe that they are all realistic and achievable, as long as I work hard with hope, truth, sincerity, and determination on my side.

Organizations to Contact

The editors have compiled the following list of organizations concerned with the issues debated in this book. The descriptions are derived from materials provided by the organizations. All have publications or information available for interested readers. The list was compiled on the date of publication of the present volume; the information provided here may change. Be aware that many organizations take several weeks or longer to respond to inquiries, so allow as much time as possible.

Advocates for Youth
2000 M Street NW, Suite 750, Washington, DC   20036
(202) 419-3420 • fax: (202) 419-1448
e-mail: information@advocatesforyouth.org
Web site: www.advocatesforyouth.org

Advocates for Youth's mission is "creating programs and advocating for policies that help young people make informed and responsible decisions about their reproductive and sexual health." Programs and initiatives such as the Teen Pregnancy Prevention Initiative and the Youth Activist Network help get young people involved in this process. The organization supports free access to birth control, including emergency contraception, for all young people. The organization's publications, many of which are free online, include fact sheets on adolescents and abortion, abstinence-only programs, and pregnancy among young teens.

American Pregnancy Helpline
(866) 942-6466
e-mail: aph@thehelpline.org
Web site: www.thehelpline.org

In addition to a toll-free telephone and e-mail hotline, the American Pregnancy Helpline provides teens and others facing an unplanned pregnancy with resources, information, and links. Offering guidance on abortion, adoption, and parenting, the site also provides pregnant teens with information about pregnancy health, early childhood, and sexual health. There is also a "guy's corner" with male perspectives on pregnancy, parenting, and sexually transmitted diseases.

Coalition for Positive Sexuality
P.O. Box 77212, Washington, DC   20013-7212
(773) 604-1654
Web site: www.positive.org

The Coalition for Positive Sexuality was formed in Chicago in 1992 as a grassroots movement made up of teenagers and several nonprofit organizations. The coalition's goal is to provide teens with unbiased, uncensored information about sexuality and to facilitate dialogue in schools and in public about contraception and sex education. The booklet *Just Say Yes* is distributed to schools and individuals, and much of its information is also available on the Web site. The coalition also produces a set of provocative posters designed to raise awareness.

Girl-Mom
Web site: www.girl-mom.com

Founded by a young mother, Girl-Mom is a resource site for young moms. Including essays, feature articles, and a positive discussion forum, Girl-Mom offers support and positive feedback for its members and visitors.

Healthy Teen Network
1501 Saint Paul Street, Suite 124, Baltimore, MD   21202
(410) 685-0410 • fax: (410) 687-0481
Web site: www.healthyteennetwork.org

Healthy Teen Network is a national nonprofit organization focused on adolescent health and well-being, focusing particularly on issues related to teenage pregnancy prevention, teen pregnancy, and teen parenting. Healthy Teen Network aims to increase awareness of these issues among health care workers, social services organizations, and the general public. Student memberships provide benefits such as reduced rates on publications, admission to an annual conference, and access to a members-only section of the Web site. Publications include evaluations of birth control and sex education courses.

Medline Plus: Teenage Pregnancy

Web site: www.nlm.nih.gov/medlineplus/teenagepregnancy
.html

Sponsored by the National Library of Medicine, MedlinePlus is a consumer health information Web site. The section about teenage pregnancy leads readers to information about health risks, sources of support, current research, and organizations. It also provides answers to frequently asked questions, as well as information on coping with becoming a teenage parent.

National Abstinence Education Association

1701 Pennsylvania Avenue NW, Suite 300
Washington, DC   20006
(202) 248-5420 • fax: (202) 580-6559
e-mail: info@abstinenceassociation.org
Web site: www.abstinenceassociation.org

Believing that the best way to prevent teenage pregnancy is to advocate for abstinence until marriage, the National Abstinence Education Association seeks to "serve, support and represent individuals and organizations in the practice of abstinence education." The association lobbies in support of expanded funding for abstinence-only education in public schools, sponsors research to support its claims, and offers training and resources for educators involved in abstinence-only programs. It has approximately 250 organizational members in 41 states.

The National Campaign to Prevent Teen and Unplanned Pregnancy
1776 Massachusetts Avenue NW, Suite 200
Washington, DC 20036
(202) 478-8500 • fax: (202) 478-8588
Web site: www.thenationalcampaign.org

The National Campaign to Prevent Teen Pregnancy was founded in 1996 with the goal of reducing the teen pregnancy rate by one-third over the next ten years. Having achieved this goal, the campaign's follow-up agenda is to reduce the rate by another one-third by 2015. The organization's mission includes expanded education about, and access to, contraception, as well as sponsoring programs that emphasize personal responsibility with regard to sexual choices. The campaign runs public service announcements on major television networks, organizes a Youth Leadership Team, sponsors the National Day to Prevent Teen Pregnancy, and advocates for public policy with members of the U.S. Congress and Senate. Its publications include *One in Three: The Case for Wanted and Welcomed Pregnancy*, *Ten Tips for Parents to Help Their Children Avoid Teen Pregnancy*, and a variety of postcards and posters to raise awareness.

National Fatherhood Initiative
101 Lake Forest Boulevard, Suite 360
Gaithersburg, MD 20877
(301) 948-0599 • fax: (301) 948-4325
Web site: www.fatherhood.org

The National Fatherhood Initiative's mission is "to improve the well-being of children by increasing the proportion of children growing up with involved, responsible, and committed fathers." The message is intended for all fathers, including those who are teenagers. Through curricula, training programs, and public service announcements, the National Fatherhood Initiative encourages fathers of all ages to be deeply involved in their children's lives. The organization produces a decision-making video game for adolescent males called "Boyz 2 Dads."

New Moms
2825 West McLean Avenue, Chicago, IL   60647
(773) 252-3253 • fax: (773) 252-5320
e-mail: contact@newmomsinc.org
Web site: www.newmomsinc.org

This Chicago-based nonprofit provides services, shelter, and training for young teen moms, many of whom were formerly homeless. Established in 1980 when its founder distributed diapers and formula to destitute young mothers, the organization has since received local, state, and federal grants and now offers housing, day care, and educational programs for young mothers and their families. Its goals include helping its participants achieve stable housing situations, teaching basic life skills, and improving the health and well-being of teen parents and their children.

Plain Talk/Hablando Claro
2000 Market Street, Suite 600, Philadelphia, PA   19103
(215) 557-4487 • fax: (215) 557-4485
Web site: www.plaintalk.org

Sponsored by the Annie E. Casey Foundation, Plain Talk/Hablando Claro's goal is to increase parent–child communication and adolescent access to contraception, thereby reducing the rate of teenage pregnancies and sexually transmitted diseases. Focused especially on low-income adolescents of color, Plain Talk/Hablando Claro provides resource materials in English and Spanish and administrative support to sites nationwide. Its newsletter, *The Communicator*, is available online.

Planned Parenthood
434 West 33rd Street, New York, NY   10001
(212) 541-7800 • fax: (212) 245-1845
Web site: www.plannedparenthood.org

Planned Parenthood, comprising more than a hundred independent organizations, is the largest reproductive health organization in the United States. Planned Parenthood–affiliated organizations offer sexual health education and affordable reproductive health services, including birth control and abortion. The organization publishes dozens of classroom sex education activities, peer education sex education programs, and other publications, including the pamphlet *Choosing Abortion: Questions and Answers.*

Project Reality
1701 East Lake Avenue, Suite 371, Glenview, IL   60025
(847) 729-3298 • fax: (847) 729-9744
Web site: www.projectreality.org

Project Reality is one of the largest abstinence-only advocacy organizations in the United States. It offers a variety of curriculum programs for students in grades 4–12. Project Reality also sponsors training programs for teachers and parents interested in abstinence-only education and maintains a roster of high-profile speakers who will discuss abstinence education for school assemblies and parent meetings. In addition, Project Reality offers teens motivational posters, bracelets, and pins reinforcing its message.

For Further Research

Books

Annie E. Casey Foundation, *2007 Kids Count Data Book*. Baltimore: Annie E. Casey Foundation, 2007.

Suzanne Cater and Lester Coleman, *Planned Teenage Pregnancy: Perspectives of Young Parents from Disadvantaged Backgrounds*. Bristol, United Kingdom: Policy Press, 2006.

Robert Coles, *The Youngest Parents: Teenage Pregnancy as It Shapes Lives*. New York: Norton, 1997.

Anne Daguerre and Corinne Nativel, *When Children Become Parents: Welfare State Responses to Teen Pregnancy*. Bristol, United Kingdom: Policy Press, 2006.

J. Shoshanna Ehrlich, *Who Decides?: The Abortion Rights of Teens*. Westport, CT: Praeger, 2006.

Tricia Goyer, *Life Interrupted: The Scoop on Being a Young Mom*. Grand Rapids, MI: Zondervan, 2004.

Ruth Graham and Sara Dormon, *I'm Pregnant . . . Now What?* Ventura, CA: Regal Books, 2004.

Laura Haskins-Bookser, *Dreams to Reality: Help for Young Moms*. Buena Park, CA: Morning Glory Press, 2006.

Helen S. Holgate, Roy Evans, and Francis K. O. Yuen, *Teenage Pregnancy and Parenthood*. New York: Routledge, 2006.

Jon Morris, *Road to Fatherhood: How to Help Young Dads Become Loving and Responsible Parents*. Buena Park, CA: Morning Glory Press, 2002.

Angelia M. Paschal, *Voices of African-American Teen Fathers: "I'm Doing What I Got to Do."* New York: Haworth Press, 2006.

Tina Radziszewicz, *Ready or Not?: A Girl's Guide to Making Her Own Decisions About Dating, Love, and Sex*. New York: Walker & Company, 2006.

Jayne E. Schooler, *Mom, Dad . . . I'm Pregnant: When Your Daughter or Son Faces an Unplanned Pregnancy*. Colorado Springs: NavPress, 2004.

Helena Silverstein, *Girls on the Stand: How Courts Fail Pregnant Minors*. New York: New York University Press, 2007.

Thomas L. Whitman, *Interwoven Lives: Adolescent Mothers and Their Children*. Mahway, NJ: Erlbaum, 2001.

Dorrie Williams-Wheeler, *The Unplanned Pregnancy Book for Teens and College Students*. Virginia Beach: Sparkledoll Productions, 2004.

Periodicals

Bill Albert, "51%: Latinas and Teen Pregnancy," *Conscience*, Summer 2007.

Kelly King Alexander, "A Mom Too Soon," *Ladies Home Journal*, April 2008.

Chloe Bland, "Unplanned Parenthood," *Teen Vogue*, December–January 2003.

Stefanie Block, "Sex(less) Education: The Politics of Abstinence-Only Education in the United States," *Women's Health Journal*, April–September 2005.

Mary C. Breaden, "Impact of Sex Education on Pregnancy Examined," *Education Week*, April 2, 2008.

Gemma Briggs, Marni Brownell, and Noralou Roos, "Teen Mothers and Socioeconomic Status: The Chicken-Egg Debate," *Association for Research on Mothering Journal*, Winter/Spring 2007.

J.E. Dahl, "Pregnancy High," *Seventeen*, May 2006.

Alexandra Rockey Fleming, "Mama Drama," *Scholastic Choices*, January 2005.

Maggie Gallagher, "Washington Encourages Teenage Pregnancy," *Forbes*, September 23, 1996.

Tricia Goyer, "When Children Have Children," *Today's Christian Woman*, July–August 2006.

Cathy Gulli, "Suddenly Teen Pregnancy Is Cool?" *Maclean's*, January 28, 2008.

Heidi L. Hallman, "Reassigning the Identity of the Pregnant and Parenting Student," *American Secondary Education* 36, Fall 2007.

Gardiner Harris, "Teenage Birth Rate Rises for First Time Since '91," *New York Times*, December 6, 2007.

Chris Hayhurst, "Childcare Programs Help Teen Parents Stay in School," www.teenwire.com, November 11, 2005. http://www.teenwire.com/infocus/2005/if-20051111 p393-childcare.php.

Linda Jacobson, "School-Based Child Care Meets Myriad Needs," *Education Week* 16, no. 18, January 29, 1997.

April Kaplan, "Teen Parents and Welfare Reform," *Welfare Information Network Issue Notes* 1, no. 3, March 1997.

Beth Kormanik, "School for Teen Parents Struggles for Relevance," *Florida Times-Union*, May 4, 2004.

Tiffany Lankes, "Teenage Parents Will Be Facing New School," *Sarasota (Fla.) Herald-Tribune*, May 6, 2008.

Molly Lopez, Jill Smolowe, and Michelle Tauber, "Teen Pregnancy Growing Up Too Fast," *People Weekly*, January 14, 2008.

Sara Neufeld, "Teaching Teen Mothers," *Baltimore Sun*, March 20, 2006.

Kaisa Raatikainen et al., "Good Outcome of Teenage Pregnancies in High-Quality Maternity Care," *European Journal of Public Health* 16, no. 2, 2006.

Mary K. Reinhart, "Teen Parent Program in Tempe Seeks Funds," *Arizona Daily Star*, September 29, 2006.

Francesca Robinson, "Targeting Teenage Pregnancy," *Practice Nurse*, February 22, 2008.

Lois S. Sadler et al., "Promising Outcomes in Teen Mothers Enrolled in a School-Based Parent Support Program and Child Care Center," *Journal of School Health* 77, no. 3, March 2007.

Arielle F. Shanok and Lisa Miller, "Stepping Up to Motherhood Among Inner-City Teens," *Psychology of Women Quarterly*, September 2007.

Cheryl Wetzstein, "Pregnancy Pause," *Washington Times*, May 25, 2006.

Kelly White, "When You Least Expect It," *Girls' Life*, February–March 2008.

Index